Eating Out

The Friendly Waiter and I

With
Charles Dickens

REG EDMONDSON · RON COOK · PETER PARK

£14.99

Contents

FOREWORD

Being a Pickwickian, I had long ago determined to follow my great-grandfather's footsteps along the coaching inns and taverns of Britain. Years ago I did it to Great Yarmouth, and more recently from Bristol to the outskirts of Birmingham. It is wonderful to be eating and drinking in the same places as did Charles Dickens, and meeting the same sort of people that he did...

It is with great pleasure that I agreed to write the Foreword to *Eating Out With Charles Dickens*. I have been encouraging the authors for many months in their zeal to find as many as possible of the old haunts still surviving.

They have done a remarkable job and are to be commended.

It is interesting to remember that Boz, as he was in 1836, wrote in *Pickwick Papers*:-

> "In the Borough especially, there still remain some half dozen old inns,
> which have preserved their external features unchanged, and have
> escaped alike the rage for public improvement, and the encroachments
> of private speculation!"

He would surely have been happy that the authors must feel the highest pleasure in laying before you, as proof of their careful attention, indefatigable assiduity, and nice discrimination, with which their search has been conducted.

They may not have explored the Hampstead Ponds or discussed Tittlebats, but they have uncovered a number of old hotels, inns and taverns visited by Charles Dickens, and which are worthy of your attention.

The fact that there are over one hundred named establishments would have pleased my revered ancestor.

I know he would have applauded the hard work and skill of our authors. May this book give you many hours of enjoyment following in his footsteps, from being a boy alone in the huge City of London, through his youth as a Parliamentary Reporter, to becoming the best-loved author and actor through his Reading Tours around Britain, Ireland and America.

Cedric Charles Dickens   13th June 2003

------- INTRODUCTION -------

When Dickens resigned from the *Morning Chronicle* in 1836 to start his second writing career as a full time novelist, it was no surprise that his first major book, *The Pickwick Papers*, was itself one of the great coaching stories. Even though stagecoaches and coaching inns were fast disappearing, Dickens deliberately set the story nine years earlier. His connection with inns and hostelries is a common thread linking his life and works and had been forged in childhood, starting when he was a boy living in Chatham and continuing to the end of his life when he went on a final trip to Limehouse to research *The Mystery of Edwin Drood*. In all that time, he'd come across every conceivable type of establishment ranging from smoky, dingy drinking dens to magnificent galleried coaching inns and, of course, the Victorian equivalent of cosy, country pubs. All left a lasting impression on Dickens, in more ways than one.

There's no doubt that childhood curiosity first drew him to this forbidden, adult world. The inns were not only at the heart of local life they were also mysterious, noisy and exciting places to be around. Dickens also enjoyed the spectacle of the horses and carriages coming and going, and the hustle and bustle that surrounded the major coaching inns. He never forgot these experiences and revisited the past time and again -- and if he couldn't go in person, he'd let one his characters make the journey. He once said that it is "a mistake to fancy that children ever forgot anything", and like so many of his early life and recollections, it's not surprising that parallels can be found throughout decades of his journalism and writing.

When the family moved to Camden in London from Kent in 1823, this marked the beginning of the unhappiest period in Dickens' young life; his father got into debt and was incarcerated at Marshalsea prison, south of the river. Dickens had to give up his education and take work in a factory at Hungerford Stairs, sticking labels on bottles of blacking. He got to know London -- and the inns and taverns -- well during this difficult time, walking miles each day to and from work to his lodgings in Lant Street and to visit his father. There's no doubt that the experience left him scarred and ashamed, but it was also a turning point: he made the decision to better himself by writing his way out of poverty. Ironically, the journey to fame and fortune would inextricably link him to the past -- and the coaching inns once more.

Dickens quickly mastered shorthand then worked as a freelancer before eventually joining the *Morning Chronicle* covering predominantly legal and political affairs. It was a time of great opportunity for any ambitious journalist trying to make a name, including Dickens. Parliament was in turmoil over constitutional change and unrest had spread; to keep his finger on the pulse and get the scoops before his rivals, he embarked on marathon trips up and down the country on assignments and for research purposes typically "writing on the palm of my hand, by the light of a dark lantern, in a postchaise and four, galloping through a wild country, all through the dead of night, at the then surprising rate of fifteen miles an hour". It could take several days just to cover a few hundred miles under horsepower, so his travels could prove long and exhausting on the bumpy, dangerous coaching roads. There were always hazards along the way too -- many of the stagecoaches were in a decrepit state -- but for Dickens, this was all part of a reporter's life.

The gigs would make their way through the countryside in all weathers and, for the occupants, including Dickens, the only respite from the tedium of travelling this way would be for frequent stopovers at a staging post, and the chance to rest, drink and dine at one of the inns that lined the coaching routes. This became a familiar routine for Dickens and one that would often be repeated.

Like any inquisitive journalist, Dickens never missed a chance to gather material, even if he couldn't use it straightaway, and there was clearly no better place to start looking for a story or to gauge public opinion than in the inns and taverns: fate had brought him full circle. Just a few years before, he had been a young boy on the outside looking in, now he relished the opportunity that these places gave him to soak up the atmosphere, listen to the tittle-tattle and, most importantly, feed his imagination with an abundance of ideas and unforgettable faces. The inns were a magnet for all sorts of people, from passers-by to pilgrims (on the Canterbury route), and continually proved useful for his fact-finding missions. It is fortuitous that he did rely on them so much for both inspiration and for practical purposes, since the coaching roads were the lifeblood of the inns and without being immortalised in print, many more would surely have disappeared.

The need to travel remained the one constant in Dickens' life, and increasingly so after the success of *Pickwick*. In a little over a year, Dickens went from obscurity amongst the literati, largely because he wrote under the pen name Boz, to prolific writer and editor. The pressure of deadlines and the demands of his publishers and adoring public alike meant there was no let-up in Dickens' hectic, gruelling schedule; he not only travelled to find people and plots for his novels, but to fulfil his obligations as one of the most fêted authors of the day. Even the prospect of going by train didn't make journeys any easier, since his literary landscapes, like his travels, spread all over the place. Although he often seemed preoccupied with the nooks and crannies of London and the Medway towns, both places close to his heart, he carried on traversing the length and breadth of Britain by various means -- including walking miles and miles on foot -- looking for material to bring to the printed page. He wasn't just travelling for work purposes either; he was in demand, both in this country and America, as a celebrity, and his popularity also enabled him to showcase his other talents doing reading tours, speeches and theatricals. He could afford to stay in the best hotels, and was on the guest list at the grandest houses, but he'd still just as happily lodge or take rooms at a coaching inn if it was more convenient -- although it became much harder for him to travel, let alone work, without being recognised. Dickens knew that his continued success depended as much on his gift of being able to write something extraordinary out of something seemingly ordinary, as it did on his creative genius. For this reason, he liked to stay close to the sharp-end of humanity and in touch with reality, which is why he did normal things, such as drinking in a seedy tavern or staying at an inn. His novels prove that he had stored ideas and notes from decades of travelling and about countless inns, and cherry-picked to suit each one.

With his eye for such "great, rambling, queer old places", it's not surprising that his works have also become a byword for defining the different inns and taverns of the 19th century; so much so, that his detailed descriptions have also provided an authoritative historical and architectural record. He was very meticulous about locations too -- many of his journeys can still be traced stage by stage -- which has also proved useful in locating inns outside the major towns or off the beaten track. Some inns are integral to the plots, particularly in *The Pickwick Papers*, *Barnaby Rudge* and *Martin Chuzzelwit*, while others reprise Dickens past. In *David Copperfield*, young David often travels by stagecoach, as Dickens did, since the novel is considered to be autobiographical. In *The Uncommercial Traveller* he describes being "packed -- like game -- and forwarded carriage paid, to the Cross Keys, Wood Street, Cheapside, London" which is a reference to his arrival in London as a ten-year-old. But he also used the inns and taverns as a literary device to set a scene, to introduce characters, to add a little "colour", and to give the reader a taste of life in Victorian times. The maxim "write about what you know about" was clearly never far from Dickens' thoughts; he writes so vividly and succinctly -- honed from years taking verbatim notes in parliamentary debates -- that apart from being able to visualise the typical "clean floor covered with crisp white sand, a well swept hearth, a blazing fire, a table decorated with white cloth, bright pewter flagons, and other tempting preparations for a well-cooked meal", it's almost possible to taste the atmosphere filled with the "fragrant odour of steaming grog and rare tobacco". Similarly, there are many wonderful purple passages just focusing on eating and drinking, plus descriptions of the characters, decor and inn signs. Other inns found their way into print for different, often personal reasons: glimpsed from a stagecoach window, perhaps a venue Dickens kept in mind after a private meal; a favourite haunt of his for a drink and chat, such as Ye Olde Cheshire Cheese in Fleet Street; an inn he chanced upon on holiday or during one of his epic walks. It must be remembered that Dickens was a sociable person and a congenial host with a wide circle of friends from all walks of life, so some inns have become famous simply because the great man frequented them -- there is sometimes no literary connection. Whatever the reasons, the purpose of this unique book is to bring this wonderful collection of places together under the Dickens umbrella.

For many years, we have been on our own culinary tour, retracing Dickens' journeys and dining at the inns, taverns and alehouses (now, of course, pubs, hotels and restaurants) with which he is associated. It became clear that this hobby could be shared with other fans -- and foodies -- and turned into the definitive guide to eating out, figuratively of course, with Dickens, Pickwick, Copperfield, and a cornucopia of misfits, madmen and murderers that he so brilliantly characterised!

However, despite Dickens' powers of observation and eye for detail, there have been difficulties with this project and the main task has been to sort out the fact from fiction; many of the inns have long gone, changed names, become private homes, or were unnamed in the narrative or purely fictional in the first place. Similarly, there have been some "pretenders" too, which have a name with a Dickens flavour but no real connection; you only have to look up and down any high street to see the impact of his characters and novels on shop signs and other premises. And just to add to the confusion, Dickens himself often used artistic licence to disguise real place names in a literary context: one example of this is Ye Old King's Head in Chigwell, Essex, mentioned in *Barnaby Rudge*. Dickens called it The Maypole, but it is known from its description and location that it is really Ye Old King's Head, which still serves a pint and a pie today. Similarly, The Grapes in Narrow Street, Limehouse -- still one of the most authentically Dickensian inns -- was called The Six Jolly Fellowship Porters in *Our Mutual Friend*; the Bull Inn in Rochester underwent three name changes, no less, first appearing as The Wingelbury Arms in *Sketches by Boz*, then under its own name in *Pickwick* to end up as the focal point for Pip's downfall as The Blue Boar in *Great Expectations*. Dickens wasn't adverse to renaming places either: in *Nicholas Nickleby*, the village of Eaton Socon, near Newark, is called "Eton Slocomb" and in *Pickwick Papers*, "Eatanswill" in Suffolk is really Sudbury. Despite all this, historians and enthusiasts have been trying to compile an erudite travelogue on Dickens for over a century, including B.W. Matz, who wrote a book on inns with a Dickens connection in the 1920s. However, much information about Dickens' movements has been lost with the passage of time and, in some cases embellished, since his name is still good for business. Dickens was a prodigious letter writer though (there are over 14,000 published ones), so his notes and missives to friends and family have proved invaluable in linking real inns with the author's pen. The scale and diversity of his travels have been well-documented in other ways too: through newspaper cuttings, advertising bills for his extensive reading tours and theatricals and, most importantly, personal papers and effects that belong to the Dickens House Museum and the Dickens family. The work of his friend and biographer (and regular travelling companion), John Forster, has also given an insight into his travels, as well as answering many of the "who, what, when, why" questions.

With the help of all these traditional sources of information this book has become a reality; researchers on the project have found over 101 of the most famous -- and genuine -- Dickensian inns for you to visit. There are many different types of establishments included, from the larger, imposing inns in the major towns and cities, such as The Angel at Bury St Edmunds, to traditional pubs with beams and blazing fires -- the choice is yours. But what they have in common, apart from Dickens, is glorious food, good service and a genuine ambience -- all the ingredients that are necessary for a fabulous meal, and not a bowl of gruel in sight! And to whet your appetite, many of the inns are crammed with Dickens memorabilia.

In this age of convenience foods and takeaways, it's good to know that there are still eateries that can combine the best of both worlds; the past and present, along with contemporary or traditional food served in surroundings reminiscent of bygone days. And when you linger over your meal with family or friends, don't forget to take a moment to look around and see the place through Dickens' eyes... I wonder which characters he would have had in mind for us?

> *"The candles were brought, the fire was stirred up, and a fresh log of wood thrown on. In ten minutes' time, a waiter was laying the cloth for dinner, the curtains were drawn, the fire was blazing brightly, and everything looked (as everything always does, in all decent English inns) as if the travellers had been expected, and their comforts prepared, for days beforehand."*
>
> "Pickwick Papers - Book II   Chapter LI

Charles Dickens' birthplace, 393 Old Commercial Road, Portsmouth.

Key to symbols

Car Parking (Private)

Car Parking (Street)

Children's Menu

Non-smoking

Smoking

Disabled Access

Garden / Play Area

Credit Cards Accepted

Amex

£   Main Dishes up to £6

££   Main Dishes up to £12

£££   Main Dishes over £12

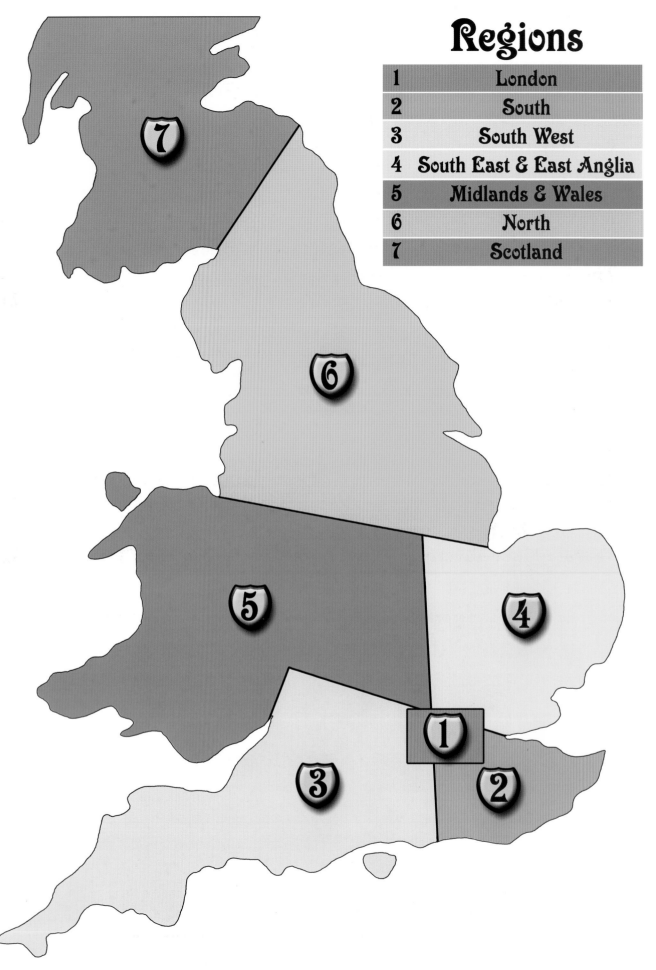

Regions

1	London
2	South
3	South West
4	South East & East Anglia
5	Midlands & Wales
6	North
7	Scotland

London

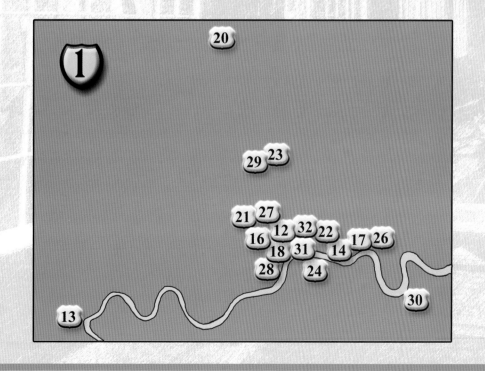

Cittie of Yorke

22-23 High Holborn
London
WC1V 6BS

Tel : 0207 2327 670

HISTORY: The Cittie of Yorke stands close to Holborn Bars, the historic entrance to the City of London where visitors going to and from the City were checked and paid their tolls. A pub has stood on this site since 1430. In 1695, it was rebuilt with a garden in front and was called Gray's Inn Coffee House. By the 1890s the building had been showing signs of decay, and was partially demolished and reconstructed in the present form; much of the old material was carefully preserved and incorporated into the present building. The great high trussed roof, the long bar counter and the fine screen work of the rearmost and largest of the three rooms, covers the area occupied by the first coffee house and contains much of the original material. The many small compartments and long row of vats ranging between 500 and 1,100 gallons, make it unique and unlike any other pub. The front bar with its more intimate atmosphere, panelling, and original chandeliers, contains the coats of arms of the Cities of York and London. The cellar bar is the old cellarage of the 17th century coffee house. Next to the pub is the gateway leading to Gray's Inn, where Charles Dickens worked as a clerk for Ellis and Blackmore; the building is still standing today.

BARS: A wide choice of hot and cold food is offered and includes special sandwiches, which are served with salad garnish and chips, and may be Cumberland sausages and fried onions on thick cut bread; toasted ciabatta with mozzarella, red pesto, olives and roast peppers; toasted Brie, bacon and pear, or regular sandwiches such as honey roast ham and mustard, Cheddar and spicy pickle. These are available with soup of the day or salad and fries. Also on the menu are jacket potatoes with a variety of fillings such as prawns in Marie Rose sauce, baked beans or chilli con carne. To round off your meal you can choose from dishes like hot apple pie, mulled wine brúlée, sticky toffee pudding or apple crumble.

OPENING TIMES:
Bars:
    Monday - Saturday   11.30am - 11.00pm
    <u>Closed on Sundays</u>
DIRECTIONS:Nearest tube Chancery Lane.

Ⓟ ⊜ ⊗ ♿ 💳 VISA 🏧   **£ - ££**

DICKENS CONNECTION

"The well-known shops, however, with their cheerful lights, did something for me; and when I alighted at the door of the Gray's Inn Coffee-house, I had recovered my spirits. It recalled, at first, that so-different time when I had put up at the Golden Cross, and reminded me of the changes that had come to pass since then; but that was natural.
"Do you know where Mr. Traddles lives in the Inn?" I asked the waiter, as I warmed myself by the coffee-room fire."

"David Copperfield"   Book II   Chpt. LIX

Coach & Horses

183 London Road
Isleworth
Middlesex
TW7 5BQ

Tel : 0208 5601 447

HISTORY: The actual date of the pub's construction is not known, but it was recorded in 1759. The Coach & Horses is a rare survivor of the numerous coach houses that once existed in the Hounslow/Isleworth district in the 17th and 18th centuries. The area was a major stopping place for coaches en route from London to the West Country. At times, as many as 500 passed through daily. A Parliamentary survey of 1650 recorded 120 inns in a one mile stretch of Hounslow High Street.

BAR: Dickens memorabilia abounds as you enter the cosy bar of this busy pub. Sit by the open fire and take your pick from the classic menu, which features "cooked to order" meals such as scampi and chips, burgers, and bangers. You can also snack on delicious sandwiches or baguettes filled with everything from B.L.T. to tuna, ham, cheese or prawns.

RESTAURANT: For something a little more contemporary and exotic, head for the Kwan Restaurant, which serves over 76 Thai dishes. To start, there's spicy Thai fish cakes served with cucumber salad and a delicate sweet and sour coriander dip or traditional Thai chicken soup flavoured with coconut milk. Mains include a vast choice of meat and poultry, seafood, fish, and vegetarian dishes. Sublime desserts to tempt you include pandon-flavoured pancakes filled with a mixture of coconut and palm sugar served with ice cream, or deep-fried banana in batter topped with honey and sesame seeds. For more traditional tastes, there is also a carvery with all the trimmings available on Sundays.

OPENING TIMES:

Bar / Restaurant:

Monday - Saturday	12.00am -	2.30pm
	6.00pm -	10.00pm
Sunday	12.00am -	4.00pm

DIRECTIONS:
A4 to Gillette corner, and then follow signs to Brentford. Close to Syon Lane British Rail.

DICKENS CONNECTION

"At length, they came to a public-house called The Coach and Horses: a little way beyond which, another road appeared to turn off. And here, the cart stopped. Sikes dismounted with great precipitation, holding Oliver by the hand all the while; and lifting him down directly, bestowed a furious look upon him, and rapped the side-pocket with his fist, in a significant manner". "Good-bye, boy," said the man. "He's sulky," replied Sikes, giving him a shake; "He's sulky. A young dog! don't mind him". "Not I!" rejoined the other, getting into his cart. "It's a fine day, after all". And he drove away."

"Oliver Twist"   Chpt. XXI

George & Vulture

3 Castle Court
Cornhill
London
EC3V 9DL

Tel : 0207 626 9710

HISTORY: The George & Vulture was an old City Chop House and is a listed building, but there has been a hostelry on the site since 1268. The tavern consists of four storeys, with two dining areas; one on the ground floor and another on the first floor. The second and third floors have rooms that are available for private parties or meetings. The Dickens Room at the top is still the meeting place for a branch of the modern-day Pickwick Club, and is also where the Dickens family have gathered together each Christmas for a meal since 1950. Charles Dickens--who used the pen name Boz--invited 34 of his friends to supper at the George & Vulture. The bill, including wine came to £11 5s. (Copy of the original bill is on page 14.)

RESTAURANT: The ground floor dining area has a typical old world appearance whereas the elegant upstairs dining room provides a more formal, intimate setting for a meal. The food offered in both is mainly classic English with chef's dishes of the day as well. There's a good choice of hot and cold starters, such as King prawns, smoked Scottish salmon, baked field mushrooms covered in a Stilton sauce, and devilled whitebait. Imaginative and well-prepared mains include a variety of special fish dishes, Dover sole and sea bass being typical, plus a selection of mixed grills and meat dishes, such as Barnsley chops or medallions of pork with caramelised apples. If you prefer more rustic fayre, opt for steak and kidney pie, calves' liver and bacon or the George's famous bubble and squeak! Finish your meal with a selection of cold sweets such as ice cream or sorbets or chef's sweet of the day.

OPENING TIMES:

Monday - Friday   12.00am - 3.00pm

DIRECTIONS: Nearest tube Bank Station.

£ - £££

DICKENS CONNECTION

"Here, the friends for a short time, separated. Messrs. Tupman, Winkle, and Snodgrass repaired to their several homes to make such preparations as might be requisite for their forthcoming visit to Dingley Dell; and Mr. Pickwick and Sam took up their present abode in very good good, old-fashioned, and comfortable quarters: to wit, the George and Vulture Tavern and Hotel, Georges Yard, Lombard Street. Mr. Pickwick had dined, finished his second pint of particular port, pulled his silk handkerchief over his head, put his feet on the fender, and thrown himself back in an easy chair, when the entrance of Mr. Weller with his carpet bag aroused him from his tranquil meditations."
"Sam," said Mr. Pickwick. "Sir," said Mr. Weller. "I have just been thinking, Sam," said Mr. Pickwick, "that having left a good many things at Mrs. Bardell's, in Goswell Street, I ought to arrange for taking them away, before I leave town again." Wery good, Sir," replied Mr. Weller."

"Pickwick Papers"   Book I   Chpt. XXVI

Lamb & Flag

33 Rose Street
Covent Garden
London
WC2E 9EB

Tel : 0207 4979 504
Fax : 0207 3797 655

> Stay traveller reft & refresh yrself in this ancient tavern within whose walls so many great figures of the past have taken their eafe. Here often sat the immortal Charles Dickens & his friends, poor Samuel Butler & the wits & gallants of the reftoration. Hither resorted the Bucks & Dandies to witness prize fights & cock mains, while hard by was enacted the notorious Rofe Alley Ambuscade in Decr 1679 when the poet Dryden was almost done to death at the instance of Louise De Keroualle, Miftrefs of Charles II.
>
> Courage & Barclays Noted Ales on Draught & Entire
>
> The Lamb and Flag

OPENING TIMES:

Bar/Restaurant:
All week   11.00am - 3.00pm

DIRECTIONS: Nearest tube Covent Garden.

⊗   £ - ££

DICKENS CONNECTION

It was Charles Dickens' 'local'.

The office where he worked on his magazine "All The Year Round" was nearby in Wellington Street.

BAR: Much of the ancient character of this tavern has been carefully preserved; low ceilings, wooden floors, wood panelling and picture curios. It has a relaxed but lively atmosphere and is very popular with office/shop workers and tourists. Traditional bar snacks are available including ploughman's, pâté, doorstep sandwiches with various fillings such as roast beef, ham and cheese plus a selection of toasted sandwiches.

RESTAURANT: The upstairs dining room offers good wholesome food which is freshly-prepared and might be soup of the day served with French bread, roast beef or lamb, toad-in-the-hole, vegetable curry and rice, or Cornish pastie. To follow, there's a list of desserts from the blackboard.

Prospect of Whitby

57 Wapping Wall
London
E1W 3SH

Tel : 0207 481 1095

HISTORY: This historic riverside inn dates back to 1520 in the reign of Henry VIII and was originally called the Devil's Tavern. It was a meeting place of sailors, and on 20th May 1553, Sir Hugh Willoughby and his crew set sail from the nearby reach in their fatal attempt to discover the north-east passage to China. At the end of the 16th century, the area became the setting for public executions, one of the most famous being Captain Kidd. It is said that Judge Jeffreys (of Bloody Assizes fame) would reputedly watch the hangings of the felons whom he had sentenced, from the balcony built over the tideway from the tavern. In 1777, it was renamed The Prospect of Whitby after a collier that was regularly moored off the tavern and was a local land-mark. Throughout history the pub has been patronised by many famous people including Charles Dickens, Samuel Pepys, Joseph Turner, and more recently by stars such as Paul Newman, Glen Ford and Rod Steiger.

BAR: The unique historic atmosphere of the pub is still preserved, and some of the fine features include a 400 year old flagstone floor and a rare old pewter bar top supported by lengths of original wooden masts, and lovely mullioned windows. There's a good choice of "Just a Bite" food, such as sandwiches, rolls, classic ploughman's and salads. Hot dishes include the usual favourites like jacket potatoes, sausages and mash, fish and chips and hearty grills. Desserts may be apple and blackberry crumble, tiramisu, and ice cream.

RESTAURANT: With its stunning views over the Thames the upstairs dining room is worth a visit for its riverside setting alone. But the food won't disappoint either, mouth-watering main courses from the à la carte menu include beef Wellington, honey and peppercorn chicken, and herb roasted salmon. Finish your meal with a choice of tempting desserts.

OPENING TIMES:
Bar:

Monday - Saturday	12.00am -	10.00pm
Sunday	12.00am -	9.00pm

Restaurant:

Monday - Saturday	12.00am -	3.00pm
	7.00pm -	11.00pm
Sunday	12.00am -	3.00pm

DIRECTIONS: Nearest tube Wapping

£ - £££

DICKENS CONNECTION

Charles Dickens regularly visited his godfather Christopher Huffam who lived nearby in Church Row (now Newall Street) and ate and drank in The Prospect of Whitby.

Rules

**35 Maiden Lane
Covent Garden
London
WC2E 7LB**

Tel : 0207 3790 258

Web : www.rules.co.uk

E-mail : info@rules.co.uk

RESTAURANT: For any literary or theatrical buff, a visit to Rules is a must. As well as Charles Dickens, the restaurant has been frequented by such greats as Graham Greene, John Betjeman and William Makepeace Thackeray -- and is still a favourite eatery amongst London's media and arts set. The restaurant serves over 500 people a day and specialises in classic British food, such as game, oysters, pies and puddings. In fact, the game is sourced from the restaurant's own estate in the Pennines, so the menu can feature more unusual choices when in season including snipe, suckling pig and partridge.   Straightforward and satisfying starters to tempt you include Morcambe Bay potted shrimps, half a dozen oysters or a slice of Stilton and walnut tart with spiced pear and apple chutney. Follow with hearty steak and kidney pie with mashed potato and a root vegetable purée or fillet of venison with a green chartreuse sauce on a mushroom and herb mash. Seafood features strongly with everything from fishcakes to roasted sea bass. Sublime puddings to tempt you include sticky toffee pudding, apple and blackberry crumble or dark chocolate pudding soufflé. There's also a week-night pre-theatre menu.

OPENING TIMES:

All week   12.00am - 12.00pm

DIRECTIONS: Nearest tube Covent Garden.

Ⓟ ⊗ ☺ 💳 VISA 📷   £ - £££

DICKENS CONNECTION

Dickens often visited the restaurant; he had an office in nearby Wellington Street, where he edited his magazine "All The Year Round".

The Avenue (Formerly The Red Lion)

**31 High Street
Barnet
EN5 5UW**

Tel : 0208 4492 667

HISTORY: Originally called The Antelope, the name changed in 1720 to The Red Lion, but it is now called The Avenue. An unsavoury incident occurred at the inn when an army officer and his daughter, passing through Barnet to London, only succeeded in obtaining accommodation after a great deal of trouble. On retiring to her room, the young lady opened a cupboard and to her horror a corpse toppled out. Apparently, the accommodation had been made by hastily removing the body from the bed and placing it where it should not have been found. This affected the inn's business for many years, and may have given Charles Dickens an idea for a story on a similar theme in *The Lazy Tour of Two Idle Apprentices Christmas Stories, Book II chapter II.*

In 1796, a Mr. Isaac Newton became the owner, the coaching trade reaching its peak during his residence, although it was set against a background of social unrest at home and war with France. Newton, as Parish Overseer of the Poor, is said to have dispensed relief to demobilised soldiers and sailors straggling through Barnet, often wounded and distressed. The Red Lion's rival at the time for the post chaise trade was the Green Man further up the High Street. Their staff, each in their own distinctive liveries, were always competing for custom. The staff at the Red Lion thought nothing of forcibly taking out the post-horses from private carriages passing by and putting in a pair of their own to do the next stage. This was free of charge in order to prevent the business going to their rival. The landlord would often give travellers a glass of sherry and a sandwich, but finding that similar offers at the Green Man were more attractive, he engaged a gang of bruisers to pounce on passing chaises and they even hauled them out of the yard at the Green Man.

This led to official intervention for the safety of travellers. The coaching era declined with the arrival of the railways in about 1862.

BAR/RESTAURANT: The high ceilings, modern decor and open-plan enhances the spacious bar and dining areas where a good choice of hot and cold snacks and main meals are available. These range from baguettes filled with chicken, tuna or cheese, and hot fillings such as sausage and onions, and steak and onions. Other options include jacket potatoes, fish and chips, lasagne, scampi, mixed grill and steaks. Desserts might be hot treacle sponge or chocolate brownie.

OPENING TIMES:

Bar/Restaurant:
All week   12.00am - 9.00pm

DIRECTIONS: Town centre near the church. Nearest tube High Barnet.

DICKENS CONNECTION

In March 1838, three days after the birth of his eldest daughter Mamie, Dickens invited John Forster, the child's godfather, to a meal at The Red Lion.

The Boot

116 Cromer Street
London
WC1H 8BS

Tel : 0207 8373 842

Some years after *(1724)*, a public-house was erected on a part of this "free land", and became charged with the annuity. It was a small and only occasionally frequented house. Charles Dickens, in "Barnaby Rudge, a tale of the Riots of Eighty,'" describes it as "The Boot Inn". *St. Pancras, Past and Present*

HISTORY: A typical London pub built in 1801 and a reminder of the London of bygone days, it now stands surrounded by modern-day buildings.

BAR: The large open plan bar has plenty of seating. One corner is devoted to Dickens books and memorabilia, making you appreciate the significance of The Boot in Dickens' novel *Barnaby Rudge*. The pub offers a wide variety of freshly-cooked food such as braised steak, lamb shank, shepherd's pie, mixed grill, lasagne with chips and salad. For a light snack, there's a choice of salads and also sandwiches with various fillings -- ham, beef or cheese.

OPENING TIMES:

Monday - Friday
and Sunday 12.00am - 9.00pm
No food served on Saturdays.

DIRECTIONS: Nearest tube and main line stations King's Cross/St. Pancras.

Ⓟ 🚻 £

DICKENS CONNECTION

"As they were thirsty by this time, Dennis proposed that they should repair together to The Boot, where there was good company and strong liquor. Hugh yielding a ready assent, they bent their steps that way with no loss of time. The Boot was a lone house of public entertainment, situated in the fields at the back of the Foundling Hospital; a very solitary spot at that period, and quite deserted after dark. The tavern stood at some distance from any high road, and was approachable only by a dark narrow lane, so that Hugh was surprised to find several people drinking there, and great merriment going on. He was still more surprised to find among them almost every face that had caught his attention in the crowd; but his companion having whispered him outside the door that it was not considered good manners at The Boot to appear at all curious about the company. He kept his council, and made no show of recognition."

"Barnaby Rudge" Book I Chpt. XXXVIII

The Centre Page (Formerly The Horn Tavern)

**29 Knightrider Street
London
EC4V 5BH**

Tel : 0207 2363 614

E-mail :
centrepage@frontpagepubs.com

HISTORY: The Horn Tavern is believed to have been founded in 1660 after King Charles II came to the throne. It is a rare survivor among old taverns of the City of London, having been rebuilt after the Great Fire of London in 1666, and surviving the Blitz of 1939-45. It was originally called The Bugle Horn, which may have been inspired by the high notes of coaching horns that echoed through the narrow streets. There were many coaching inns around St. Paul's during this period. Records show that many famous people frequented the tavern, including the great diarist, Samuel Pepys, Horace Walpole and many other Tory politicians. In 1775, when John Wilkes, the radical politician and rake was Master of the Joiner's Company, he ordered wine for the Company's refreshment at The Horn Tavern after taking part in the procession on Lord Mayor's Day. It was also a coffee house where newspapers could be read and the headlines of the day discussed. The Horn survived a threat of demolition in 1967 after a campaign was organised to save it.

BAR/DINING ROOM: There's a warm and lively atmosphere in the modern style interior where a wide choice of freshly-prepared international dishes are served such as white bean, fennel and rosemary soup with black olive bread, or nachos with melted cheese, sour cream and salsa. Main courses include North African lamb with chilli, ginger, chickpea and cous cous; haddock, mussels, leek and cider pie; duck, dried fruits and Pinot Noir sausages with tarragon mashed potatoes and red wine jus. There's an interesting selection of salads and pasta dishes, as well as sandwiches such as bacon, lettuce and tomato on a muffin served with fries, and tuna or egg mayonnaise. Delicious puddings such as Bailey's crème brúlée, chocolate brownies, or a selection of cheese and biscuits complete your meal.

OPENING TIMES:

Bar/Dining Room:

Monday - Friday	12.00am -	3.00pm
Saturday	12.00am -	9.00pm
Sunday	12.00am -	8.00pm

DIRECTIONS: Nearest tube St. Paul's.

Ⓟ ♯♯ ☺ ⊗ ▭ ▭ ▭ £ - ££

DICKENS CONNECTION

"Mr. Weller produced upon the little dining table, a roast leg of mutton and an enormous meat pie, with sundry dishes of vegetables, and pots of porter, which stood upon the chairs or the sofa-bedstead, or where they could, everybody felt disposed to do justice to the meal, notwithstanding that the meat had been purchased and dressed, and the pie made, and baked, at the prison cookery hard by.
To these, succeeded a bottle or two of very good wine, for which a messenger was dispatched by Mr. Pickwick to the Horn Coffeehouse, in Doctors' Commons. The bottle or two, indeed, might be more properly described as a bottle or six."

"Pickwick Papers"   Book II   Chpt. XLIV

The Flask

77 Highgate West Hill
Highgate
London
N6 6BU

Tel : 0208 3487 346

Web : www.theflaskhighgate.co.uk

HISTORY: The original building was a school dating from 1663; the first reference to it being a public house was in 1716. It was later extended and what is now the main bar was originally cottages and this part of the building dates from 1760. The Flask was at one time called the Upper Bowling-Green House due to the fact that it had a very good bowling green. In the garden there was a mulberry tree under which you could drink your ale. It was a meeting place of the Kit Kat Club. They originally held meetings at the Cat & Fiddle in the City; the shop of a pastry cook named Christopher Kat. They were Whig Patriots who at the end of King William's reign met in out-of-the-way places to devise measures to secure the Protestant Monarchy and keep out the Catholic Stuarts. Latterly, they assembled for simple enjoyment and regularly met at The Flask. The name originates from flasks that were obtainable here to collect the famous Hampstead Wells mineral water. Twice a year, the ceremony of "Swearing on the Horns" is enacted, which is an old Highgate custom. Travellers passing through the village must take part in the ceremony with the mayor being present on these occasions. This involves the individual kissing a pair of horns which are secured to a pole and then reciting the oath.

BAR: The bar has a warm and cosy atmosphere with alcoves where you can relax and enjoy a wide choice of freshly-prepared food. This ranges from light bites such as curried pumpkin and sweet potato soup, smoked mackerel, cucumber and red onion bruschetta, roast beef or ham sandwiches, to farmhouse cheese platter. Main courses include pan -fried calves' liver with bubble and squeak, and a tangy red onion gravy; oven-roasted Moroccan lamb rump on a bed of couscous with roasted butternut squash.   Mouth-watering home-made puds such as chocolate brownie with crème fraiche, or bread and butter pudding, complete your meal.

OPENING TIMES:
Bar/Restaurant:

Monday - Saturday	12.00am -	3.00pm
	6.00pm -	10.00pm
Sunday	12.00am -	4.00pm
	6.00pm -	9.30pm

DIRECTIONS:
Nearest tube Archway/Highgate.

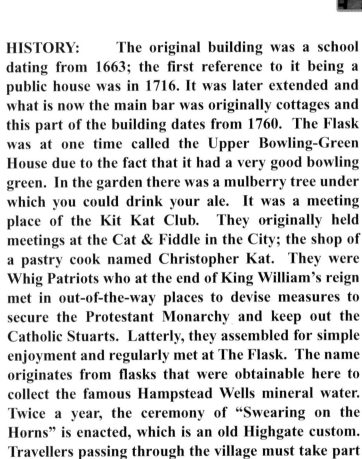

DICKENS CONNECTION

"I had engaged a bed at a decent alehouse close by, and was going out at the gate, when, happening to turn my head, I saw a light in the Doctor's study. A half-reproachful fancy came into my mind, that he had been working at the Dictionary without my help. With the view of seeing if this were so, and, in any case, of bidding him good-night, if he were yet sitting among his books, I turned back, and going softly across the hall, and gently opening the door, looked in, the first person I saw, to my surprise, by the sober light of the shaded lamp, was Uriah. He was standing close beside it, with one of his skeleton hands over his mouth, and the other on the doctor's table."

"David Copperfield"   Book II   Chpt. XLII

The George Inn

77 Borough High Street
Southwark
London
SE1 1NH

Tel : 0207 4072 056
Fax : 0207 4036 613

HISTORY: The George is London's only surviving galleried coaching inn and overlooks a quaint cobbled courtyard. The original inn was destroyed in the Great Southwark Fire of 1676 and was rebuilt the following year. Until the 18th century, the only way coaches could cross the Thames was over London Bridge, which had a curfew imposed at sunset stopping people from entering the city, leaving tired and hungry travellers on the Southwark side of the river. To cater for their needs, many inns were built along Borough High Street. Next door to The George was The White Hart, where Charles Dickens first introduces Sam Weller in *Pickwick Papers*. However, in the great railway boom of the 19th century most of these inns declined. Guy's Hospital, then owners of The George, sold it to the London and North Eastern Railway Company, who demolished a great portion to make way for warehousing, leaving just the south side which remains today. In good weather, players perform extracts from Shakespeare's plays in the courtyard. The ground floor is divided into several bars; one used to be the waiting room for coachman and passengers, and contains an Act of Parliament clock dating back to 1797 when Parliament put a tax on timepieces, and the other bar was the coffee room. Today, the inn's future is safe in the hands of The National Trust.

BARS: The ground floor bars are very cosy with low beamed ceilings, bare-board floors and lattice windows, and serve mainly traditional pub food including baguettes and rolls with a choice of fillings, soup of the day; jacket potatoes; steak, mushroom and Guinness pie, sausage and mash, fried fish or pasta. For something light, try the continental salad bowl with a choice of prawns, chicken, beef or ham and a chunk of baguette. Sweets include apple pie, and delicious hot treacle sponge.

RESTAURANT: An impressive stairway leads up to the first-floor restaurant full of old world charm, where the same traditional food is available.

OPENING TIMES:

Monday - Saturday		
Bar	12.00am -	3.00pm
Restaurant	12.00am -	2.30pm
	6.00pm -	9.00pm
Sunday		
Bar/Restaurant	12.00am -	4.00pm

DIRECTIONS: London Bridge Station or Monument. About 100 yards down Borough High Street.

£ - ££

DICKENS CONNECTION

"And if Mr. Tip - if he happens to be a coming in as I come out, and if he says, 'Where are you going, Maggy'? and if I says, "I'm a going So and So", and if he says, "I'll have a try too", and if he goes into The George and writes a letter, and if he gives it to me and says, "Take that one to the same place, and if the answer's a good 'un I'll give you a shilling", it ain't my fault mother!,
Arthur read, in little Dorrit's downcast eyes, to whom she foresaw that the letters were addressed."
"Little Dorritt" Book I Chpt. XXII

25

The Grapes

76 Narrow Street
Limehouse
London
E14 8BP

Tel : 0207 9874 396
Fax : 0207 9873 137

HISTORY: The history of this pub can be traced back to 1585, the 27th year of the reign of Queen Elizabeth Ist. Henry, Lord Wentworth, leased nine parcels of waste ground from his manor at Limehouse. Thus began the story of The Grapes. It is in the year 1704 that we have reference to the premises being used for the sale of alcoholic beverages. The building, along with its neighbours, apparently burned down in 1718, but they were rebuilt around 1720. As a young boy, Charles Dickens would have known this area as he frequently visited his godfather, Christopher Huffam, who sold oars, masts and ships' gear in Church Row (now Newell Street), which is just around the corner from The Grapes.

BAR: The long, narrow beamed bar with half-wood panelled walls and etched glass windows extends to a small balcony with fine views of the river. The many pictures of Dickens' characters add to the unique atmosphere. Club sandwiches, smoked salmon, ploughman's, plus soup, and hot dishes such as bangers and mash, poached salmon, and homemade desserts are served daily. A traditional English roast is also served at lunchtime on Sundays.

RESTAURANT: The award-winning restaurant specialises in delicious seafood, which comes from Billingsgate each morning. Catch of the day may include favourites such as Dover sole, supreme of halibut, sea bass, plus more contemporary and unsual combinations. However, orders for "specials" like lobster, oysters, crayfish and other exotic fish must be made 24 hours in advance. There's an extensive choice of starters and puddings to complement the main courses -- if you've got room!

OPENING TIMES:

Bar:

Monday - Friday	12.00am -	2.00pm
	7.00pm -	9.00pm
Saturday	12.00am -	2.30pm
	7.00pm -	9.00pm
Sunday	12.00am -	3.00pm

Restaurant:

Monday - Friday	12.00am -	2.15pm
	7.30pm -	9.15pm
Saturday	7.30pm -	9.15pm

The Restaurant is closed on Sundays.

DIRECTIONS:
Docklands Light Railway Westferry Road. Near Limehouse Basin turn off A1203.

DICKENS CONNECTION

"The Bar of the Six Jolly Fellowship Porters was a bar to soften the human breast. The available space in it was not much larger than a hackney-coach; but no one could have wished the bar bigger, that place was so girt in by corpulent little casks, and by cordial bottles radiant with fictitious grapes in bunches, and by lemons in nets, and by biscuits in baskets."

"Our Mutual Friend"   Chpt. VI
Dickens called "The Grapes" "The Six Jolly Fellowship Porters"

The Lamb

94 Lamb's Conduit Street
Bloomsbury
London
WC1N 3LZ

Tel : 0207 4050 713

Web : www.youngs.co.uk

HISTORY: Dating back to the 18th century, the pub was named after the engineer, Sir William Lamb, who built the conduit, which was originally an Elizabethan dam made in one of the tributaries of the Fleet River to bring clean water to local households. Sir William also provided 120 buckets for the poorest people to carry the water in. The conduit has long gone, but there is a charming statue of a lady with an urn in Guildford Place at the top of the street which bears his name. The Lamb was a meeting place for members of the Bloomsbury Set which included Leonard and Virginia Woolf.

BAR/RESTAURANT: The striking horseshoe bar with its original set of etched-glass "snob-screens", which pivot at face level, were used in Victorian times to shield the pillars of society when they were drinking with women of dubious distinction and did not wish to be observed from the public bar. The wood-panelled walls are decorated with a display of Hogarth prints and sepia photographs of stars of the Victorian music halls and theatres. In the unique setting of living history, you can enjoy a large selection of freshly -prepared food ranging from light bites such as breaded mushrooms, smoked salmon with brown soda bread and butter, traditional ploughman's lunch or fish and chips. Main dishes can include shepherd's pie, liver with bacon and onions, sirloin or gammon steaks served from the griddle.

OPENING TIMES:

Monday - Saturday	12.00am -	2.30pm
	6.00pm -	9.00pm
Sunday	12.00am -	2.30pm

DIRECTIONS: Nearest tube Russell Square/Chancery Lane.

DICKENS CONNECTION

Charles Dickens would have used The Lamb as his local whilst living in nearby Doughty Street in 1837.

The Red Lion

48 Parliament Street
London
SW1A 2NH

Tel : 0207 9305 826
Fax : 0207 9307 860

HISTORY: The present building stands on the site of a medieval tavern that was known in 1434 as The Hopping Hall, and later as The Rose and eventually the Red Lion. The carcass of the present building dates back to 1733, but it has been much altered and was remodelled in 1896 by Architects Shoebridge & Rising to cater for a very superior clientele. The pub is one of a number in the environs of Parliament to have a division bell to summon MPs back to the House of Commons when a vote is imminent. Above the second floor window there is a stunning carved plaque of Charles Dickens.

BAR: You can choose from a delicious selection of freshly-prepared sandwiches with a choice of fillings until about 8.00pm. Jacket potatoes are also served and other snacks can be found on the blackboard.

RESTAURANT: In the attractive dining room with its carved wood panelling and ceiling decorated with "Vanity Fair" characters and Parliamentary memorabilia, a good variety of traditional food is available which is freshly-cooked to order, including roast of the day, lasagne, steak and kidney pie, fish and chips, and salads. To finish, try one of the home-made desserts.

OPENING TIMES:

Bar/Restaurant:

Monday - Saturday   12.00am - 3.00pm

<u>Light snacks available up to 8pm.</u>

DIRECTIONS: Nearest tube Westminster.

£ - ££

DICKENS CONNECTION

"I remember one hot evening I went into the bar of a public-house, and said to the landlord; "What is your best - your very best-ale a glass?" For it was a special occasion. I don't know what. It may have been my birthday. "Twopence-halfpenny," says the landlord, "Is the price of the Genuine Stunning ale." "Then," says I, producing the money, "Just draw me a glass of the Genuine Stunning, if you please, with a good head to it."

"David Copperfield"   Book I   Chpt. XI

The event probably occurred in 1823 when Charles Dickens was eleven years old.

The Spaniards Inn

Spaniards Road
Hampstead
London
NW3 7JJ

Tel : 0208 7316 571

HISTORY: The inn was originally built in 1585 as a country house for the Spanish Ambassador to the Court of James Ist. By the mid 18th century it was opened as an inn by two Spanish brothers. Many famous artistic and literary figures are known to have visited the inn including Percy Bysshe Shelley, John Keats, Lord Byron and, of course, Charles Dickens. In 1780, a band of rioters led by Protestant Lord George Gordon, stopped at the inn before marching to the home of Catholic Lord Mansfield which was nearby. However, soldiers arrived and they were arrested and marched off to Newgate jail.
(Gordon Riots: Protestants were suspicious that there was a Catholic plot to put a Catholic on the throne and replace Protestant, King George III.)

BAR: With its low ceilings, uneven floors, and old straight high-backed benches, you step back in time. Old pictures adorn the walls and you can sit in the cosy alcoves and enjoy a wide choice of freshly-prepared food. Dishes range from humous and pitta bread, soup of the day, a selection of sandwiches on ciabatta bread, to main dishes like braised lamb shank and mash, chicken, leek and mushroom pie, or Mrs. O'Keeffe's handmade wild boar sausages and mashed potato. On Sunday's, there's a choice of roast ribs of beef or roast chicken. You can also eat upstairs in a beautiful wood-panelled room. Haagen Dazs ice cream, tarte tatin, crème brúlée tartlet, are some of the puddings available. In the summer, you can sit in a lovely garden, where there is delightful aviary.

OPENING TIMES:

Bar:

Monday - Friday	12.00am -	3.00pm
	5.00pm -	9.00pm
Saturday - Sunday	12.00am -	5.00pm

DIRECTIONS:
Nearest tube Golder's Green.

£ - £££

DICKENS CONNECTION

"The party walked forth, in quest of a Hampstead stage. This was soon found, and in a couple of hours they all arrived safely in the Spaniards Tea-gardens, where the luckless Mr. Raddle's very first act nearly occasioned his good lady a relapse; it being neither more or less than to order tea for seven, whereas (as the ladies one and all remarked), what could have been easier than for Tommy to have drank out of anybody's cup - or everybody's, if that was all - when the waiter wasn't looking; which would have saved one head of tea, and the tea just as good! However, there was no help for it, and the tea-tray came, with seven cups and saucers, and bread and butter on the same scale. Mrs. Bardell was unanimously voted into the chair, and Mrs. Rogers being stationed on her right hand, and Mrs. Raddle on her left, the meal proceeded with great merriment and success."

"Pickwick Papers"   Book II   Chpt. XLVI

Trafalgar Tavern

Park Row
Greenwich
London
SE10 9NW

Tel : 0208 8582 437
Fax : 0208 8582 507

HISTORY: There has been an inn on the site of the Trafalgar Tavern since the mid 1700s, probably much longer. It was originally called The George Inn but became known as Old George by 1805. With the opening of the new railway line from London in the 1830s and the number of steam 'packets' plying the river, Greenwich was booming and it was decided the premises should be extended. The new building was opened in 1837 and was called the Trafalgar Tavern. In the 1800s Greenwich became renowned for its whitebait.   Cabinet Ministers of the day had established a habit of holding regular "Whitebait Dinners" and the Trafalgar soon became the favourite venue for William Gladstone and the "Whigs", and this lasted until the turn of the century. Due to increased competition, the Trafalgar closed in 1915. It was used successfully as an institution for merchant seamen, a working men's club, and flats. Watney's Brewery restored and re-opened the Trafalgar as a pub in 1965. Currently, the pub welcomes today's Cabinet Ministers and The Saints and Sinners Club of London for their annual Whitebait Dinner - although the whitebait no longer comes from the Thames.

BAR/RESTAURANT: The Regency building has impressive bay windows giving spectacular views; it has a spacious and relaxing atmosphere, with a fine collection of celebrity pictures which include Charles Dickens and William Makepeace Thackeray. There is a very large choice of food, with the emphasis on fresh seafood such as oysters, prawns, mussels and freshly delivered fish and, of course, whitebait. There's a wide choice of starters such as herbed goat's cheese and beetroot roulade, char-grilled squid or tempura

vegetables basket. For something a little lighter, try the Trafalgar salad, which is cornfed chicken breast, smoked bacon, dressed leaves, garlic croutons, Parmesan cheese, topped with whitebait. Main meals include steak and mushroom pie, sausages and mash, char-grilled rib eye steak. To complete your meal, try one of the sublime desserts such as tarte tatin, raspberry crème brûlée or chocolate truffle cake.

OPENING TIMES:
Bar:
    Monday - Sunday   12.00am - 2.30pm

Restaurant:
    Tuesday - Saturday   12.00am - 9.30pm

DIRECTIONS: Docklands Light Railway to Canary Wharf, change for Greenwich. Situated near Royal Naval College.

Ⓟ ⊗ ⊜ ♿ ▭▭ £ - £££

DICKENS CONNECTION

"What a dinner! Specimens of all the fishes that swim in the sea, surely had swum their way to it, and if samples of the fishes of divers colours that made a speech in the Arabian Nights (quite a ministerial explanation in respect of cloudiness), and then jumped out of the frying-pan, were not to be recognised, it was only because they had all become one hue by being cooked in batter among the Whitebait."

"Our Mutual Friend"   Book II   Chpt. IV

Ye Olde Cheshire Cheese

**Wine Office Court
145 Fleet Street
London
EC4A 2BU**

Tel : 0207 3536 170
Fax : 0207 3530 845

E-mail :
cheshirecheese@compuserve.com

HISTORY: The site originally formed part of a 13th century Carmelite Monastery and there has been a pub here since 1538. The present house was built following the Great Fire of London in 1666, and is one of the few remaining 17th century chophouses. Pictures and artefacts throughout the building portray the people, events and history of the almost 350 years the Cheshire Cheese has existed. Charles Dickens was a frequent customer when he worked on the *Daily News,* as were, amongst other famous people, Oliver Goldsmith and Dr. Samuel Johnson.

BARS: The Cellar Bar and the Cheshire Bar have a wonderful atmosphere with their wooden bays provided by high-backed church pews and long oak tables. You can enjoy a good selection of traditional dishes including a daily specials board of home-cooked hot food, plus the usual tempting favourites like jacket potatoes and ploughman's. If you're part of a large group, dip into a mixed platter of garlic mushrooms, chicken nuggets, potato wedges and other savouries. Quick and tasty options include rustic bread sandwiches.

RESTAURANT: The Johnson Restaurant serves more substantial meals, which can include starters such as smoked salmon and dill terrine, or duck and port pâté with Cumberland sauce. Main dishes feature firm favourites like steak and kidney pudding, Scotch roast beef with all the trimmings, and fish and chips. There's also a choice of chicken, pork and lamb dishes. Tempting desserts include lemon meringue pie, dark chocolate fudge cake, and sticky toffee pudding.

OPENING TIMES:

Restaurant:			
Monday - Friday	12.00am	-	3.00pm
	6.00pm	-	9.30pm
Bars:			
Monday - Friday	12.00am	-	9.30pm
Saturday	12.00am	-	3.00pm
	6.00pm	-	9.30pm
Sunday	12.00am	-	3.00pm

DIRECTIONS:
Nearest tube Temple/Chancery Lane.

DICKENS CONNECTION

"Drawing his arm through his own, he took him down Ludgate Hill to Fleet Street, and so, up a covered way into a tavern. Here, they were shown into a little room, where Charles Darnay was soon recruiting his strength with a good plain dinner and good wine; while Carton sat opposite to him at the same table, with his separate bottle of port before him".

"A Tale of Two Cities" Chpt. IV

Ye Olde Mitre Tavern

1 Ely Court
Ely Place
Charterhouse
London
EC1N 6SJ

Tel : 0207 4054 751

HISTORY: The recorded story of Ely Place and Ely House goes back to the 13th century in the time of Bishop Kirkby, and it was early in the 14th century that a palace was built and became the town residence of the Bishops of Ely, in Cambridgeshire. When you enter Ely Court with its narrow passageways, you are transported from the hustle and bustle of modern day London to an historic little pub untouched by time. The first Mitre Tavern was built in 1546 by Bishop Goodrich for the house servants, and there is a mitre bearing this date outside the present building. It was in 1576 that Sir Christopher Hatton, the 'dancing' favourite of Queen Elizabeth Ist practically commandeered the house from Bishop Fox. Hatton was granted 21 years' lease of a large part of the house and ground. His rent was one red rose, ten loads of hay and £10 annually. In the Mitre bar parlour is the preserved trunk of a cherry tree around which Elizabeth Ist is reputed to have danced the maypole. In Shakespeare's Richard II, Ely House is where John of Gaunt made his famous 'sceptered isle' speech. One important liberty still left to the residents of Ely Place is freedom from entry by the police, except by invitation.

BAR: Over the past 400 years the atmosphere of this charming Elizabethan pub has changed little. To this effect, you'll find no gaming machines or music. The pub offers good-quality snacks such as toasted sandwiches with a choice of fillings, pork pies, scotch eggs and sausages. To support its membership of the Guild of Master Cellarmen, the pub serves a variety of well-kept real ales.

OPENING TIMES:

Bar:
> Monday - Friday   11.00am - 9.30pm
> <u>Closed at weekends.</u>

DIRECTIONS:
Nearest tube Chancery Lane.

DICKENS CONNECTION

"I found, when I did open it, that it was a very kind note, containing no reference to my condition at the theatre. All it said was, "My dear Trotwood. I am staying at the house of papa's agent, Mr. Waterbrook, in Ely-place, Holborn. Will you come and see me to-day, at any time you like to appoint? Ever yours affectionately, Agnes."

"David Copperfield" Book I Chpt. XXV

Dickens knew Ely Place well as he worked in Covent Garden and probably drank in the Mitre Tavern on many occasions.

South

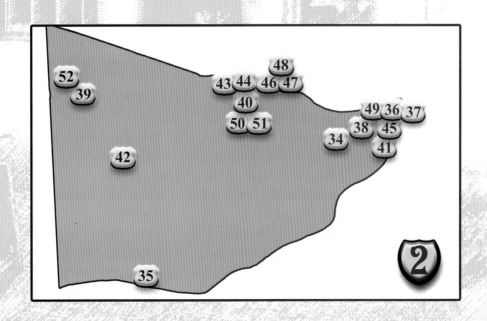

The Crown Inn

Cherry Brandy House
Sarre
Birchington
Kent   CT7 0LF

Tel : 01843 847808
Fax : 01843 847914
E-mail : crown@shepherdneame.co.uk

PATRONISED BY
CHARLES DICKENS
CRUICKSHANKS
RUDYARD KIPLING
LORD CARSON
VISCOUNT ROTHERMERE
ELLEN TERRY
LADY WYNDHAM
Sir JOHN HARE
W.H. BERRY
LIONEL BROUGH
JACK PAYNE
HERMAN FINCK
A.B. PAYNE
Col ELLIOTT ROOSEVELT
NORMAN M. SCOTT

HISTORY: The Crown Inn is a listed building of architectural and historical interest, and it is said that there has been an inn on this site since 1500. When the Huguenots were expelled from France in the 17th century many settled in Kent, and one of them bought this ale house. When he saw the fruit orchards in the area, he remembered his family recipe for cherry brandy, and so began a tradition that lasts to this day. The cherry brandy made and sold at The Crown was so popular that the inn became known as "The Cherry Brandy House", and the availability of this delicious liqueur was a requirement of the licence! This brandy is still made to a secret recipe, bottled and labelled by hand, but is now made at the Shepherd Neame Brewery at Faversham. It is only available at The Crown Inn at Sarre, and nowhere else. The inn has a rich history. A priest hole was discovered in the roof space during rebuilding. In the restaurant, a montage commemorates the fact that survivors of the "Charge of the Light Brigade" held their reunion dinners at the inn. On the front of the inn, there's a list of some of the famous people who have visited or stayed here, including Charles Dickens and his illustrator, George Cruikshank.

BAR: The cosy bar has low-beamed ceilings and displayed above the bar are many pictures of the coaches that stopped at The Crown. Around the walls, there are photographs of show business stars who have visited the inn, and this is no doubt due to the fact that the landlord at the time had previously been the manager of The Theatre Royal, Drury Lane, London. On the menu, there's a choice of lighter options such as soup of the day served with a crusty roll, tuna and cheese melt or calamari and feta cheese. Main dishes may be chef's curry of the day, lasagne, or farmhouse sausages and mash. Fish dishes include catch of the day, deep-fried and served with chips, or mussels cooked in garlic,

white wine and parsley. Freshly-made sandwiches and daily "specials" are also served at lunch time.

RESTAURANT: The charming and intimate restaurant has adjoining dining areas with pictures and memorabilia displayed around the walls, especially relating to Dickens. There's an à la carte menu with a wide choice of dishes. Starters may be pear and Stilton salad, baked stuffed mushrooms, or king prawns wrapped in filo pastry. Mains include duck breast served with a kumquat sauce, prime Scotch fillet steak or whole baked seabass filled with limes, coriander and lemon grass. Also on the menu, "specials" such as tortilla wraps, spaghetti bolognase, and chef's risotto. Irresistible desserts include panna cotta, cheesecake, Dutch apple flan, lavish ice creams and the cheese board. Don't forget to try the cherry brandy!

OPENING TIMES:
Bar:
Monday - Saturday	12.00am -	2.30pm
Sunday	12.00am -	4.00pm

Restaurant:
Monday - Saturday	7.00pm -	9.30pm
Sunday	7.00pm -	9.00pm

DIRECTIONS: On A28 between Ramsgate and Canterbury head to village centre.

£ - £££

DICKENS CONNECTION
Charles Dickens stayed at The Crown Inn en route to and from his holiday home at Broadstairs.

The Old Ship Hotel

**Kings Road
Brighton
East Sussex
BN1 1NR**

Tel : 01273 329 001
Fax : 01273 820 718

Web :
www.paramount-hotels.co.uk

E-mail :
oldship@paramount-hotels.co.uk

HISTORY: Occupying a prominent position overlooking the beach and promenade, the Old Ship dates back to 1559. In the 19th century, the Prince Regent regularly visited the hotel and it became a favourite haunt for the aristocracy and celebrities. In 1831, the great violinist Paganini performed at the hotel. The atmospheric old wine cellars with their vaulted ceilings, are now used for small private functions, but in earlier days were thought to have been used by smugglers to hide contraband.

BAR: The recently refurbished bar has views overlooking the seafront, and is a comfortable and relaxing place if you just want a quick snack. Choose from a good selection of delicious freshly-made sandwiches, hot soup of the day or maybe a crisp green salad.

RESTAURANT: The stylish Redz Brasserie has an airy and relaxed atmosphere and offers mouth-watering dishes from around the world. Starters may be cream of celeriac soup with queen scallops and mangetout, or buffalo mozzarella and vine cherry tomatoes. Main courses include bouillabaisse, minted slow roasted lamb shank, or you can cook your own fillet steak on a South African hot-rock--served with tiger prawns, French fries or salad. Chicken, venison, fish and pasta together with a variety of salads are also available. Delicious puddings include lemon tart, French apple flan, sorbets and ice cream, plus the cheese board.

OPENING TIMES:
Bar/Restaurant:

All Week	12.00am - 2.30pm
	6.00pm - 9.30pm

DIRECTIONS: A23 to seafront then take A259 Kings Road towards West Pier.

£ - £££

DICKENS CONNECTION

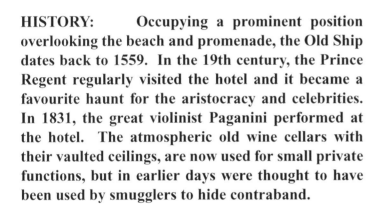

My Dear Kittenmoles,
I passed your house on Wednesday - being then atop of the Brighton Area - but there was nobody at the door, saving a solitary poulterer, and all my warm-hearted aspirations lodged in the goods he was delivering.-No doubt you observed a peculiar relish in your dinner. That was the cause.
I send you the MS. I fear you will have to read all 5 slips, but the subject I think of, is at the top of the last, where the guest, with his back towards the spectator, is looking out of the window, I think, in your hand, it will be a pretty one.
Then, my boy, when you have done it, turn your thoughts (as soon as other engagements and prostrations will allow) first to the outside of the Warren - secondly, to the outside of the locksmith's house by night. Put a penny pistol to Chapman's head, and demand the blocks of him.
I have addled my head with writing all day, and have barely wit enough left to send my love to my cousin, and-here's a genealogical poser-what relation of mine may the dear little child be at present, I desire to be commended to her clear blue eyes.

Letter written by Dickens to Mrs. A. M. Stern whilst staying at Old Ship Hotel on the 26th February 1841.

The Royal Albion Hotel

Albion Street
Broadstairs
Kent
CT10 1AN

Tel : 01843 868 071
Fax : 01843 861 509

Web :
www.albionbroadstairs.co.uk

E-mail :
enquiries@albionbroadstairs.co.uk

HISTORY: The Royal Albion was built in 1760 and stands on the seafront overlooking beautiful Viking Bay. Charles Dickens was a regular visitor during the summer months. He had the highest regard for the landlord, and it would appear the feeling was mutual. He wrote; "Mr. Ballard of the Albion Hotel - one of the best and most respectable tradesmen in England. He has a kind of reverence for me."

BAR/LOUNGE: Ballard's Lounge has recently been tastefully refurbished and every table has a sea view. There's also an adjoining terrace overlooking the bay where you can dine al fresco. A large choice of hot and cold snacks are available, which include jacket potatoes, baguettes filled with scampi and haddock fillets, and special sandwiches made from continental bread with a choice of fillings.

RESTAURANT: The Marchesi Restaurant was established in 1886, and is still run today by the great grandsons of the original owner. It has built a reputation over the years for good food and an excellent selection of fine wines. There is a set lunch and dinner menu consisting of two or three courses with a good variety of starters and main meals. The à la carte menu has a wide choice of dishes with something to suit all tastes, with starters such as fresh asparagus in puff pastry with hollandaise, and chicken and duck liver pâté. Main courses may be whole Dover sole, roast cannon of lamb with herb crust, and pork fillet in a cream and grain mustard sauce. If you

have room, there's a large choice of moreish desserts to tempt your taste buds.

OPENING TIMES:
Lounge:
All week	8.00am - 11.00pm

Restaurant:
All week	11.00am - 3.00pm
	5.30pm - 9.00pm

DIRECTIONS:
A256 to town centre. Hotel is at the bottom of the High Street.

CHARLES DICKENS. LIVED HERE 1839, 1840, 1845, 1849 & 1859. AND WROTE PART OF NICHOLAS NICKLEBY.

🚗 🚭 ☺ 💳 💳 £ - £££

DICKENS CONNECTION

Charles Dickens stayed at the hotel during the summers of 1839, 1840, 1845, 1849 and 1859.

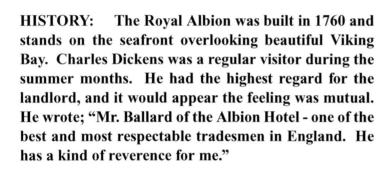

36

The Tartar Frigate

37 - 39 Harbour Street
Broadstairs
Kent
CT10 1EU

Tel : 01843 862 013
Fax : 01843 862 013

HISTORY: Built in the 16th century in an idyllic position overlooking the harbour, The Tartar Frigate is the only flint built public house on this part of the coast, and is the focal point of Broadstairs Harbour. It was the haunt of smugglers, customs men and seafarers, and has enjoyed continuous trading for more than 300 years. Old Henry, the pub's friendly ghost, is seen lurking in the shadows from time to time, and is said to have watched over this hostelry and its guests for over three centuries.

BAR: The cosy bar serves a choice of light snacks which include home-made soup, ploughman's and a selection of tasty freshly-made sandwiches with a variety of different fillings; or, you can just drop in for a pint and enjoy the view!

RESTAURANT: Under the old oak beams of this charming restaurant, which specialises in fresh seafood, diners can enjoy a wide range of international dishes. You'll find many imaginative starters, which might be cricket ball crab, Whitstable oysters, moules mariniére, avocado, raspberry and Brie salad, to soup of the day. The menu offers some interesting main courses such as lobster thermidor, bass fillets with a saffron sauce, Dover sole, monkfish, or skate. There's also a choice of sirloin and fillet steaks served with a variety of sauces, as well as chicken, duck and rack of lamb. A wide selection of desserts is available plus an extensive wine list.

OPENING TIMES:
Bar:

Monday - Saturday	12.00am -	2.00pm
Sunday	12.00am -	3.30pm

Restaurant:

Monday - Saturday	12.00am -	1.45pm
	7.00pm -	9.30pm
Sunday	12.00am -	3.30pm

DIRECTIONS:
Follow signs to harbour/seafront.

£ - £££

DICKENS CONNECTION

"Looking at them, you would say that surely these must be the laziest boatmen in the world. They lounge about, in obstinate and inflexible pantaloons that are apparently made of wood, the whole season through. Whether talking about the shipping in the Channel, or gruffly unbending over mugs of beer at the public-house, you would consider them the slowest men. The chances are a thousand to one that you might stay here for ten seasons, and never see a boatman in a hurry. A certain expression about his loose hands, when they are not in his pockets, as if he were carrying a considerable lump of iron in each."

"Reprinted Pieces" - Our English Watering-Place.

The Dickens Inn at the House of Agnes

71 St. Dunstans Street
Canterbury
Kent
CT2 8BN

Tel : 01227 472 185
Fax : 01227 464 527

HISTORY: The Dickens Inn at the House of Agnes is one of the loveliest Tudor buildings in Canterbury, situated close to the ancient West Gate. Dating back to the 16th century, this old residence is scheduled as a building of special historic interest, and is recommended in American tourist magazines as a place to visit while holidaying in the U.K. It is believed to be one of the oldest buildings in the City. Modern facilities have been installed but care has been taken to retain the unique ambience, charm and character of the building.

RESTAURANT: The food on offer in the quaint oak-panelled eatery is all made using fresh produce and includes pâté on hot toast served with a crisp, leaf salad, baked mushrooms soaked in garlic. You can also choose juicy prawns or smoked salmon. Main courses may be pepper steak in a creamy sauce, tuna fish steak, or duck in a fruits of the forest sauce. All the desserts are home-made and are changed frequently, and include old English favourites like treacle tart, chunky apple crumble or spotted dick and custard.

OPENING TIMES:
Restaurant:

All week	12.00am - 2.00pm
	6.00pm - 10.00pm

£ - ££

DICKENS CONNECTION

"Arrived at Mr. Wickfield's house, I found, in the little lower room on the ground floor, where Uriah Heep had been of old accustomed to sit, Mr. Micawber plying his pen with great assiduity. He was dressed in a legal-looking suit of black, and loomed, burly and large, in that small office. Mr. Micawber was extremely glad to see me, but a little confused too. He would have conducted me immediately into the presence of Uriah, but I declined.

"I know the house of old, you recollect," said I, "and will find my way up-stairs. How do you like the law, Mr Micawber?". "My dear Copperfield," he replied. "To a man possessed of the higher imaginative powers, the objection to legal studies is the amount of detail which they involve. Even in our professional correspondence."

"David Copperfield"   Book II   Chpt. XXXIX

DIRECTIONS:
M2/A2 to town centre; near the West Gate.

The George

**46 Guildford Street
Chertsey
Surrey
KT16 9BA**

Tel : 01932 886 781

HISTORY: The building dates back to 1364, when it was an old hunting lodge in the Windsor Great Park. The first mention of it being an inn was in 1613 when it may have been called The Prince's Arms. However, it was certainly called The Boot by 1771, but has been named The George since 1794. It is a listed building and the oldest still standing in Chertsey, retaining much of its original structure. The pub is said to be haunted by the ghost of a monk who had sinned and then hung himself. The last manifestation was in the 1960s, when a married couple staying in the pub with their friend the landlord, declared that the atmosphere in their bedroom became very tense and cold; apparently, the bed had sunk down in the middle as if someone had thrown their weight upon it!

BAR/RESTAURANT: With the wealth of oak beams and open fires, the pub has preserved much of its character. There's an extensive lunch menu of mainly wholesome English food, including a large selection of sandwiches and baguettes with fillings such as cheese, egg mayonnaise, ham, bacon, lettuce and tomato, smoked salmon and pan-fried minute steak; and also a traditional ploughman's. Hot dishes include home-made lasagne, omelettes, roast chicken, steak and kidney pudding, plus an all-day breakfast. Traditional roasts are available on Sundays, with a choice of starter and dessert.

OPENING TIMES:

Bar/Restaurant:
Monday - Saturday   11.00am - 2.30pm

Sunday   12.30pm - 3.30pm

DIRECTIONS: Take M25 to J11 then follow signs to town centre.

🚗 ⊗ ☺ **£ - ££**

DICKENS CONNECTION

"Here he paused, and looked about for the inn. There were a white bank, and a red brewery, and a yellow town hall; and in one corner there was a large house, with all the wood about it painted green; before which was the sign of "The George." To this he hastened, as soon as it caught his eye. He spoke to a postboy who was dozing under the gateway; and who, after hearing what he wanted, referred him to the ostler; who after hearing all he had to say again, referred him to the landlord; who was a tall gentleman in a blue neckcloth, a white hat, drab breeches, and boots with tops to match, leaning against a pump by the stable-door, picking his teeth with a silver toothpick."

"Oliver Twist" Chpt. XXXIII

Ye Olde Leather Bottle

**The Street
Cobham
Kent
DA12 3BZ**

Tel : 01474 814 327
Fax : 01474 812 086

HISTORY: In the pretty village of Cobham opposite the church stands an attractive half-timbered inn. It was built in 1629 during the reign of King Charles Ist, and was a royalist meeting place during the English Civil War. Around 1720 the inn became known as Ye Olde Leather Bottle, after a leather bottle containing gold sovereigns was found on the premises. The pub is renowned throughout the country for its close association with Charles Dickens and Dickensian memorabilia, with original paintings, etchings and prints covering the walls in abundance.

Standing outside the Leather Bottle is an ancient stone inscribed with the following letters

```
       +
B I L S T
    U M
  P S H I
   S. M.
  A R K
```

To solve the mystery you will have to read *Pickwick Papers - Chapter XI*

BAR: The heavily-beamed bar has a warm and inviting atmosphere and offers a good choice of hot and cold snacks such as ploughman's, hot baguettes filled with gammon and cheese, sausages or rump steak and onions, all served with chips; plus sandwiches, jacket potatoes, omelettes and a selection of salads.

RESTAURANT: The charming dining room serves mainly traditional English food which is freshly-cooked to order. To start, there's breaded mushrooms served with a choice of dips, and home-made soup of the day. Main meals may be mixed grill, salmon tail fillets with béarnaise sauce, minted lamb chops, and liver and bacon. You'll find a daily choice of "specials" featured on the blackboards on the walls. To finish your meal, there's a range of tempting desserts.

OPENING TIMES:

Bar/Restaurant:
All week   12.00am - 2.30pm
               6.00pm - 9.30pm

DIRECTIONS:
Take A2 and follow signs for Cobham.

£ - £££

DICKENS CONNECTION

"And really," added Mr. Pickwick, after half an hour's walking had brought them to the village, "really, for a misanthrope's choice, this is one of the prettiest and most desirable places of residence I ever met with."
In this opinion also, both Mr. Winkle and Mr. Snodgrass expressed their concurrence; and having been directed to the Leathern Bottle, a clean and commodious village ale-house, the three travellers entered, and at once inquired for a gentleman of the name of Tupman. "Show the gentlemen into the parlour, Tom", said the landlady, a stout country lad opened a door at the end of the passage, and the three friends entered a long, low-roofed room, furnished with a large number of high-backed leather-cushioned chairs of fantastic shapes, and embellished with a great variety of old portraits and roughly-coloured prints of some antiquity."

"Pickwick Papers" Book I Chpt. XI

Charles Dickens called "The Leather Bottle" "The Leathern Bottle"

40

The Royal Hotel

Beach Street
Deal
Kent
CT14 6JD

Tel : 01304 375 555
Fax : 01304 372 270

Web : www.theroyalhotel.com

HISTORY: Steeped in history, the elegant Royal Hotel (formerly known as The Three Kings) stands in a prominent position on the seafront overlooking the English Channel. Over the years, the hotel has offered its hospitality to the many Lords Warden of the Cinque Ports and they have included such famous figures as the Duke of Wellington, William Pitt, Queen Victoria and Sir Winston Churchill. Renowned former patrons also include Admiral Lord Nelson and his friends Sir William and Lady Emma Hamilton. In 1818, the German Princess Adelaide stayed at the hotel whilst on her way to marry the future King William IV and he permitted the Three Kings to change its name and display the monarch's crest.

BAR: The attractive bar offers a very wide range of imaginative snacks such as fresh mussels served in garlic, white wine and cream; vegetable and olive paella; chorizo sausage in tomato, peppers olive and garlic sauce; whitebait with lemon, plus extras such as garlic bread, chips and salads.

RESTAURANT: The elegant dining room has an unequalled position overlooking the sea, and has table d'hôte and à la carte menus as well as chef's "specials" which make use of fresh, seasonal produce. The innovative starters can be pan-fried quail with puy lentils and a truffle vinaigrette; game terrine wrapped in bacon on a beetroot and onion chutney, or a pear and Stilton salad with a pine nut and herb dressing. Main courses are created as complete dishes and include cannon of venison with braised red cabbage, dauphinoise potatoes and a duo of sauces, and fillet of Aberdeen Angus with pomme neuf and béarnaise sauce. There's a good choice of home-made desserts which are changed weekly and combine old favourites with exciting new flavours.

OPENING TIMES:

Bar/Restaurant:
Tuesday - Sunday   12.00am - 2.00pm
Lunch

Monday - Saturday   6.00pm - 9.15pm
Dinner
<u>Closed Sunday evening
and Monday lunchtime.</u>

DIRECTIONS: Take the A258 to seafront.

DICKENS CONNECTION

"But when we got into a warm room in an excellent hotel, and sat down, comfortably washed and dressed, to an early breakfast (for it was too late to think of going to bed), Deal began to look more cheerful. Our little room was like a ship's cabin, and that delighted Charley very much. Then the fog began to rise like a curtain; and numbers of ships, that we had no idea were near, appeared."

"Bleak House"   Book II   Chpt. XLV

The White Horse

High Street
Dorking
Surrey
RH4 1BE

Tel : 0870 400 8282
Fax : 0130 688 7241

Web :
www.heritage-hotels.com

E-mail :
whitehorsedorking@heritage-hotels.co.uk

HISTORY: First reported as an ancient vicarage in 1278, it was granted to the Hospitallers and named the Cross House in honour of their insignia. In 1750 it was established as an inn, parts of which date back to the 15th and 16th centuries. It is said to be one of the finest examples of a coaching inn in England, and there is a positively Dickensian flavour about this attractive old building, both inside and out.

BAR/LOUNGE: There's a comfortable and welcoming bar and lounge area with its open log fires in the winter months. A good selection of sandwiches are served all day as well as various hot and cold dishes, such as filled jacket potatoes, ploughman's, pasta, fish, chicken or steak. If you like something a little hotter, try the turkey or prawn curry. Morning coffee and traditional afternoon tea is also available.

RESTAURANT: The charming dining room with its low oak beams serves mainly traditional dishes, with starters such as smoked chicken terrine, or slices of seasonal melon with raspberry sauce and lemon sorbet. Main courses may be pan-fried lambs' liver and bacon, grilled venison sausages, breast of chicken and fish of the day. To finish, desserts include blueberry crème brulée, gáteau, ice cream and sorbets.

DIRECTIONS:
Leave M25 J9 and take A24 towards Leatherhead/ Dorking. The White Horse Hotel is in the town centre.

OPENING TIMES:

Bar:

Monday - Saturday	10.00am	- 2.30pm
	6.30pm	- 11.00pm
Sunday	11.30am	- 3.30pm
	6.30pm	- 11.00pm

Restaurant:

Monday - Saturday	12.00am	- 2.00pm
	7.00pm	- 9.30pm
Sunday	12.30pm	- 2.00pm

£ - £££

DICKENS CONNECTION

"He'll be as far gone in rum and water as ever he wos at the Markis o'Granby, Dorkin', and that's not sayin' a little neither." And with this, Mr. Weller once more laughed immoderately, and once more relapsed into a state of partial suffocation, in consequence. nothing could have been more in accordance with Sam Weller's feelings, then the projected exposure of the real propensities and qualities of the red-nosed man; and it being very near the appointed hour of meetings the father and son took their way at once to Brick Lane."

"Pickwick Papers" Book II Chpt. XXXIII
Dickens called the "The White Horse" "The Marquis of Granby"

The White Hart

High Street
Greenhithe
Kent
DA9 9NN

Tel : 01322 382 074
Fax : 01322 370 049

HISTORY: The White Hart is a 15th century Thame-side inn, which has been altered many times over the centuries, but still retains much of its charm and character. Originally, the rear of the inn that faces the river was the entrance, as most customers arrived by boat. Sir John Franklin, the great explorer, stayed at the inn prior to his voyage to find the Northwest Passage.

BAR: The bar has a lovely ambience with an open fire and beams, and many interesting exhibits on the walls of naval themes and connections e.g. a display of naval knots. You'll find a good selection of staple English dishes on the menu such as omelettes, jacket potatoes, sandwiches, and sausages, egg and chips.

RESTAURANT: The stylish first-floor dining room has a three-course menu with favourite starters such as prawn cocktail, stuffed mushrooms, and soup. Main courses include lamb shank, steak Diane, Cumberland sausages, fish, and lasagne, with a choice of desserts and ice cream or cheese and biscuits.

OPENING TIMES:

Bar:

Monday - Saturday	12.00am -	2.30pm
Sunday	12.30pm -	3.30pm

Restaurant:

Monday - Saturday	6.00pm -	9.00pm
Sunday	12.30pm -	3.30pm

DIRECTIONS: Follow the A2 to the Queen Elizabeth II. bridge, then take the A226 to the village.

DICKENS CONNECTION

"He put his pipe back in his mouth with an undisturbed expression of face, and sat as composed and contented as if we were already out of England. Yet he was as submissive to a word of advice as if he had been in constant terror, for, when we ran ashore to get some bottles of beer into the boat, and he was stepping out, I hinted that I thought he would be safest where he was, and he said, "Do you, dear boy?" and quietly sat down again. The air felt cold upon the river, but it was a bright day, and the sunshine was very cheering. The tide ran strong, I took care to lose none of it, and our steady stroke carried us on thoroughly well. By imperceptible degrees, as the tide ran out, we lost more and more of the nearer woods and hills, and dropped lower and lower between the muddy banks, but the tide was yet with us when we were off Gravesend."

"Great Expectations" Chpt. LIV

Sir John Falstaff

Gravesend Road
Higham
Kent
ME3 7NZ

Tel : 01634 717 104

HISTORY: The Sir John Falstaff hostelry on the old London/Dover road is named after a character in Shakespeare's play Henry IV. For hundreds of years the Dover road was used by pilgrims to and from Canterbury; by ambassadors, royals, couriers and merchants, and regiments of soldiers on their way to Gravesend. Later, in the 18th/19th centuries, as many as seventy or eighty coaches, private carriages and mail-carts passed by daily. The area was notorious for highwaymen as there were a lot of rich pickings. After the long climb up from Rochester, the horses were tired and thirsty and would stop to drink from the trough, which still remains, and coaches and passengers made an easy target. Between June and September 1856, Dickens used the Falstaff as an occasional home while major reconstruction work was carried out on his house, especially a deep well being dug in his garden. He also used the inn to accommodate guests if there was no spare room at his house, where they could, in his words, be housed "quite snugly". A few days after Dickens' death in 1870, a traveller having made a pilgrimage to Gad's Hill, and while dining at the Falstaff, said to a waiter: "A great loss, this of Mr. Dickens." "A very great loss to us, sir," replied the waiter shaking his head. "He had all his ale sent in from this house." A landlord at the Falstaff was called Mr. Trood, which might have suggested to Dickens the name "Drood".

BAR: The large open-plan bar with a cosy fire in the winter offers a good choice of hot and cold food like assorted sandwiches, baguettes with choice of fillings, omelettes, jacket potatoes and home-made pies and puddings.

RESTAURANT: The comfortable and pleasant dining room offers an exciting à la carte menu with many unusual dishes such as kangaroo and ostrich steaks with delicious sauces, and wild boar or grilled black bream. More conventional dishes can be starters such as deep-fried crab claws, mushrooms in garlic and white wine cream sauce. Main courses include steak Diane, plum roast duck or poached salmon. Home-made desserts might be chocolate fudge cake, pavlova or apple pie.

DIRECTIONS:
On A226 between
Rochester and
Gravesend.

OPENING TIMES:

Bar/Restaurant:
All week   11.30am -   2.15pm
               7.00pm -   9.45pm

£ - £££

The Belle Vue

Pegwell Road
Pegwell Bay
Ramsgate
Kent
ET11 0NJ

Tel : 01843 593 991

HISTORY: Dating back to the 1600s the Belle Vue has magnificent views overlooking Pegwell Bay. Its location made the tavern an ideal haunt for smugglers, the most famous being the local blacksmith Big Jim, who ran a notorious gang. Queen Victoria and her mother the Duchess of Kent made a visit, and also many former television stars including Tony Hancock and John Le Mesurier.

BAR/BRASSERIE: The tavern has recently been refurbished and the downstairs area offers varied brasserie-style food, with light dishes such as bruschetta, to main courses including honey and balsamic roasted salmon, lemon sole, scampi, as well as old favourites like steak and kidney pie, and a choice of delicious desserts which are changed daily.

RESTAURANT: The delightful Brummels Restaurant on the first floor offers a choice of starters such as mussels, devilled kidneys or stuffed mushrooms. There's some exciting and unusual main courses, which includes wild boar, ostrich steaks, salmon or guinea fowl. All dishes are served with a selection of fresh vegetables. Tempting, well-prepared desserts include brandysnap baskets, and peach brummel.

DIRECTIONS:
From Ramsgate take A256 to Pegwell Bay.

OPENING TIMES:

Bar/Brasserie:

Monday - Saturday	12.00am - 2.30pm	
	7.30pm - 9.30pm	
Sunday	12.00am - 3.00pm	

Restaurant:

Monday - Saturday	7.30pm - 10.00pm
Sunday	12.00am - 3.00pm

£ - £££

DICKENS CONNECTION

"Mr. & Mrs. Tuggs, and the captain had ordered lunch in the little garden behind: - small saucers of large shrimps, dabs of butter, crusty loaves, and bottled ale. The sky was without a cloud; there were flower-pots and turf before them; the sea, from the foot of the cliff, stretching away as far as the eye could discern anything at all; vessels in the distance with sails as white, and as small, as nicely-got-up cambric handkerchiefs. The shrimps were delightful, the ale better, and the captain even more pleasant than either. Mrs. Captain Waters was in such spirits after lunch! - chasing, first the captain across the turf, and among the flower-pots; and then Mr. Cymon Tuggs and then Miss. Tuggs; and laughing, too, quite boisterously."

"Sketches by Boz" Book II Chpt. IV
The Tuggs at Ramsgate.

Mr. Tope's

**60 High Street
Rochester
Kent
ME1 1JY**

Tel : 01634 845 270
Fax : 01634 845 270

MR. TOPE'S

THIS WAS THE HOME OF MR. TOPE, THE CHIEF VERGER OF THE CATHEDRAL IN "THE MYSTERY OF EDWIN DROOD". IT IS THE LAST BUILDING MENTIONED IN THE WRITINGS OF CHARLES DICKENS.

HISTORY: Standing near to the great Norman castle and the impressive old cathedral, Mr. Tope's is a 15th century building in the centre of Rochester on the old London to Dover coaching road. At the end of the 19th century the building was used as a dairy.

BISTRO BAR: Low ceilings, old oak beams and cosy fires help to enhance the old world charm of the bistro where a large variety of hot and cold food is available, and includes a selection of sandwiches, baguettes and Panini breads, plain or toasted with fillings such as tuna mayonnaise, ham and tomato, and smoked salmon, all served with a salad garnish and crisps. There's a choice of filled jacket potatoes and ploughman's with either Cheddar, pâté, ham or Stilton. Main courses have starters such as garlic mushrooms, pâté and toast, and also soup, followed by Bolognese topped with Parmesan; chicken and mushroom stroganoff, cod and chips, Kentish sausages, and succulent steaks.

RESTAURANT: The first-floor dining room offers an interesting à la carte menu with starters such as crispy duck salad tossed in mixed salad leaves infused with a raspberry dressing, and chilled prawn and avocado cocktail bound in a light seafood sauce topped with fresh crab. Main courses may be roasted rump of lamb wrapped in puff pastry served with garlic and thyme sauté potatoes, Madeira sauce and garnished with baby vegetables; red Thai vegetable curry served with timbale of mixed rice and freshly-toasted garlic naan bread; or poached roulade of smoked haddock and cod wrapped in paper thin salmon resting on potato dauphinoise with a lemon chive butter sauce. On Sundays, a roast is also served.

OPENING TIMES:

Bistro:
  All week   11.45am - 6.00pm
Restaurant:
  All week   6.00pm - 10.00pm

DIRECTIONS: A2 to town centre.

Ⓟ ♦♦ ☺ ⊗ 💳 VISA £ - £££

DICKENS CONNECTION

"Mr Tope's official dwelling, communicating by an upper stair with Mr. Jasper's (hence Mrs. Tope's attendance on that gentleman), was of very modest proportions, and partook of the character of a cool dungeon. Its ancient walls were massive, and its rooms rather seemed to have been dug out of them, than to have been designed beforehand with any reference to them. The main door opened at once on a chamber of no describable shape, with a groined roof, which in its turn opened on another chamber of describable shape, with another groined roof: their windows small, and in the thickness of the walls. These two chambers, close as to their atmosphere, and swarthy as to their illuminations by natural light, were the apartments which Mrs. Tope had so long offered to an unappreciative city."

"The Mystery of Edwin Drood"   Chpt. XVIII

The Royal Victoria & Bull Hotel

High Street
Rochester
Kent
ME1 1PX

Tel : 01634 846 266
Fax : 01634 832 312

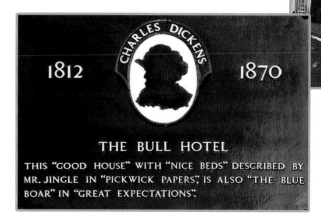

1812   1870

THE BULL HOTEL

THIS "GOOD HOUSE" WITH "NICE BEDS" DESCRIBED BY
MR. JINGLE IN "PICKWICK PAPERS", IS ALSO "THE BLUE
BOAR" IN "GREAT EXPECTATIONS".

OPENING TIMES:

Restaurant:
  All week   12.00am - 2.30pm
                      7.00pm - 10.00pm

Closed Wednesdays

DIRECTIONS: M2/A2 to town centre.

🚗 ⊗ ⊜ 💳 💳 £ - £££

HISTORY: Standing close to the ruins of the great Norman castle and Rochester Cathedral, The Royal Victoria and Bull is a 400 year old coaching inn which has been extended over the years. It stands on the old London to Dover coaching road that once ran through Rochester High Street. The hotel was originally called The Bull and it acquired its present name after Queen Victoria paid a visit in 1836. Much of the original building is still preserved -- in particular a fine staircase, the entrance hall and the ballroom.

RESTAURANT: The recently refurbished Southern Bull Restaurant has an informal and pleasant atmosphere. The menu offers a wide choice of dishes including lots of Southern spices; starters include king prawns, marinated in chilli oil and wrapped in smoked bacon, and deep-fried Camembert with a cranberry dip. Main dishes may be sirloin and fillet steaks, swordfish or salmon. If you like something hot and spicy, try the classic chilli, which is served with sour cream, rice and tortilla chips or Cajun chicken skewers. There's also a selection of pasta dishes and crisp salads, plus a wide choice of desserts.

DICKENS CONNECTION

"and the stranger continued to soliloquise until they reached the Bull Inn, in the High Street, where the coach stopped."

~~~~~~~~~~~~~~~~~~~~~~

"What's that? he inquired, as the waiter removed one of the covers. "Soles, sir." "Soles - ah! - capital fish - all come from London - stage-coach proprietors get up political dinners - carriage of soles - dozens of baskets - cunning fellows. Glass of wine, Sir." "With pleasure," said Mr. Pickwick; and the stranger took wine, first with him, and then with Mr. Snodgrass, and then with Mr. Tupman, and then with Mr. Winkle."

"Pickwick Papers"   Book I   Chpt. II

8 London Road
Stroud
Rochester
Kent
ME2 3HT

Tel : 01634 719 912

HISTORY: This grade II listed building dates back to 1437 when it was a wine shop, but the site has been occupied since 1203. The pub has been known as the Crispian and Crispianus since 1556; the name originates from the patron saint of shoemakers and was once the meeting place of the Guild of Shoemakers. The story goes that two brothers had fled to these shores to pursue their Christian religion after being persecuted by the Romans. They settled in Faversham plying their trade as cobblers and also preaching the Christian faith before moving on and suffering martyrdom. In about 1903, the landlady recalls a story that Charles Dickens was looking out of the window onto the street when a poor weary woman with two children limped by. He called them inside and paid for their refreshments and sent them on their way, happy with a shilling or two. He often frequented the pub while on one of his long walks from his home at Gad's Hill Place.

BAR: Charles Dickens would still recognise the bar today, as it is still much as he would have seen it. Among the many fine features are heavy beams and a large old fireplace. The walls are covered with brasses and prints of Dickens characters. There is a plaque above what is believed to have been Dickens' favourite seat. The bar offers a selection of light snacks, crisps and nuts.

OPENING TIMES:

Bar:
   All week   12.00am - 5.00pm

DIRECTIONS:
A2 to Rochester; at bottom of Strood Hill.

DICKENS CONNECTION

"Then, should we make a burst to get clear of the trees, and should soon find ourselves in the open, with the town-lights bright ahead of us. So should we lie that night at the ancient sign of Crispin and Crispanus, and rise early next morning to be betimes on tramp again."

"The Uncommercial Traveller"   Chpt. XI Tramps.

The Grove Ferry Inn

Grove Ferry Road
Upstreet
Nr. Canterbury
Kent
CT3 4BP

Tel : 01227 860 302
Fax : 01227 860 929

HISTORY: Situated in an idyllic location on the banks of the River Stour, the inn dates back to 1831 and was originally a coaching house. It took its name from a hand-drawn ferry that took people across the river. The ferry operated up until 1960, but records go back to 1606 -- the fare for a foot passenger was just one penny! The inn played host to Queen Victoria and later on to King George VI who visited adjacent Stodmarsh Reserve for duck-shooting. Stodmarsh is now an important conservation area, with a nature trail, picnic site and easy access routes through the reserve. In the 19th century, it is believed the inn was used as a hide-out for smugglers carrying goods across the marshes.

BAR: The attractive bar area is great if you want to dine on a variety of freshly-prepared snacks and main courses including sandwiches, ploughman's, jacket potatoes, home-cooked gammon served with chips and egg, lasagne or wholetail scampi. There's also a daily "specials board" plus a selection of delicious desserts. In fine weather, food can be eaten in the garden or on the patio terrace overlooking the river.

RESTAURANT: Cosy candlelit tables and log fires in the winter add to the friendly relaxed atmosphere. The à la carte menu has a wide range of classic dishes. Starters include soup of the day, seafood in a creamy white wine sauce, or avocado salad with hot bacon dressing. Main meals can be pan-fried calves' liver and pancetta served on a sage mash and red wine gravy; baked seabass with roasted red peppers, tomatoes and anchovies, plus seasonal specials. Tempting treats for pudding include home-made cheesecake, rhubarb crumble, sorbet and ice cream.

OPENING TIMES:

Bar/Restaurant:

Monday - Saturday	12.00am - 10.00pm
Sunday	12.00am - 9.00pm

DIRECTIONS:
Just off the A28 approximately six miles from Canterbury.

£ - £££

DICKENS CONNECTION

Charles Dickens often visited the inn whilst on his many journeys to the Kent coastal resorts for holidays.

Five Pointed Star

**100 High Street
West Malling
Kent
ME19 6NE**

Tel : 01732 842 192

HISTORY: A former farmhouse of some size, the Five Pointed Star stands in the middle of the pretty village of West Malling. On the coat of arms of the former occupants of the then manor house, now Douces Manor, is depicted a Five Pointed Star. A market house and market cross stood in front of the pub until they were demolished in 1764. In the 1960s, the pub was frequented by U.S. Navy personnel when the nearby airfield -- on loan from the RAF -- was used by the Americans. It is said to be haunted by one of the ghosts from St. Leonard's Tower; the last sighting was in 1950. On the back of the previous issue £10 note, a cricket match is depicted. This is the game between All Muggleton v. Dingley Dell from Charles Dickens' novel *Pickwick Papers*. Muggleton is the name Dickens gave to West Malling.

BAR: The bar and dining area has wooden floors, blazing log fires in the winter months, beams and many pictures of the locality around the walls, which creates a charming rustic atmosphere where you can enjoy a very comprehensive selection of hot and cold food, choose from sandwiches and French sticks with fillings such as prawns, cheese, beef or chicken; open sandwiches served with salad coleslaw and crisps; double decker hot sandwiches filled with bacon, lettuce and tomato or jumbo sausage and onions. There's also a large choice of filled jacket potatoes. Main meals offer something to suit all tastes from home-made pies filled with steak and kidney or chicken and mushroom; mixed grills, chilli-con-carne to fish and chicken dishes. To complete your meal, tempting desserts are available such as banoffee pie, triple chocolate pudding, creamy cheesecake with apple, finished off with a deliciously rich strudle crumble and caramel.

OPENING TIMES:

Bar:

Monday - Saturday	10.30am -	9.30pm
Sunday	12.00am -	9.00pm

DIRECTIONS:
M20 J4. Follow signs to town centre.

DICKENS CONNECTION

"Well; and how came you here?" said Mr. Pickwick, with a smile in which benevolence struggled with surprise.
"Come," replied the stranger - "stopping at Crown - Crown at Muggleton - met a party - flannel jackets - white trousers - anchovy sandwiches - devilled kidneys - splendid fellows - glorious."
Mr. Pickwick was sufficiently versed in the stranger's system of stenography to infer from this rapid and disjointed communication that he had, somehow or other, contracted an acquaintance with the All-Muggletons, which he had converted, by a process peculiar to himself, into that extent of good-fellowship on which a general invitation may be easily founded. His curiosity was therefore satisfied, and putting on his spectacles he prepared himself to watch the play which was just commencing. All-Muggleton had the first innings; and the interest became intense when Mr. Dumkins and Mr. Podder, two of the most renowned members of that distinguished club, walked bat in hand."

"Pickwick Papers"   Book I   Chpt. VII
Dickens called "The Five Pointed Star" "The Crown"

The Swan

**35 Swan Street
West Malling
Kent
ME19 6JU**

Tel : 01732 521 910
Fax : 01732 522 898

E-mail : fishboneltd@aol.com

HISTORY: The Swan is a 19th century coaching inn with a modernised front on a much earlier, probably 16th century, timber-framed structure. It was the posting house, and the two coaches, The Balloon and The Tally Ho, left from here daily for London. The street was originally called Holyrood Street. The name of the inn and the street originated from the fact that before the road was bridged, there was a splash at the bottom of the slope and swans were often seen swimming there. The staircase is an outstanding feature of the interior. Charles Dickens is said to have stayed here and watched cricket on the cricket field. Each July, there is a wonderfully authentic Dickensian carnival and street market in the town to commemorate his visit on which he based his famous All Muggleton v. Dingley Dell cricket match.

BAR/RESTAURANT: The bistro has a relaxed and informal atmosphere with its stylish decor, and offers a good choice of modern European cuisine dishes are prepared from the finest quality produce with something to suit all tastes, such as grilled ciabatta with melted Brie and grilled pepper, salmon and haddock fishcake with mixed salad; roasted langoustines and steamed mussels, herb butter and potato salad, and char-grilled ribeye steak with béarnaise sauce and big chips. There's an array of home-made desserts such as raspberry and mascarpone brulée, dark chocolate and kahlua torte, warm brioche pudding, all complemented by an extensive wine list. In fine weather, you can dine al fresco in the garden.

OPENING TIMES:
Lunch:
   Monday - Saturday   12.00am - 2.30pm
Dinner:
   Monday - Saturday   6.00pm - 10.30pm
Sunday Brunch:
Deli Menu   12.00am - 4.00pm
                    4.00pm - 9.30pm

DIRECTIONS:
M20 J4. Follow signs to town centre.

Ⓟ 🚭 ⊖ ♿ 🚲   ⬤ VISA   £ - £££

DICKENS CONNECTION

"There being no further preliminaries to arrange, the company straggled into town in little knots of twos and threes; and within a quarter of an hour were all seated in the great room of the Blue Lion Inn, Muggleton - Mr. Dumkins acting as chairman, and Mr. Luffey officiating as vice. There was a vast deal of talking and rattling of knives and forks, and plates; a great running about of three ponderous headed waiters, and a rapid disappearance of the substantial viands on the table; to each and every of which item of confusion, the facetious Mr. Jingle lent the aid of half-a-dozen ordinary men at least.   When everybody had eaten as much as possible, the cloth was removed, bottles, glasses, and dessert were placed on the table; and the waiters withdrew to "clear away," or in other words to appropriate to their private use and emolument whatever remnants of the eatables and drinkables they could contrive to lay their hands on."

"Pickwick Papers"   Book I   Chpt. VII
Dickens called "The Swan" the "Blue Lion Inn"

Ye Harte & Garter Hotel

High Street
Windsor
Berkshire
SL4 1PH

Tel : 01753 863 426
Fax : 01753 830 527

HISTORY: The hotel stands opposite Windsor Castle and the nearby River Thames and dates back to the middle 19th century. However, there was an inn on the site as far back as the 17th century which was frequented by people from the theatrical profession. It was the setting for a scene in William Shakespeare's *The Merry Wives of Windsor*. The hotel has been carefully restored to retain its Victorian elegance combined with modern-day facilities.

BAR: Le Café Bar has unrivalled views of the ramparts of Windsor Castle and the hustle and bustle of modern day Windsor. It is a lovely place to relax and enjoy an extensive range of freshly-cooked snacks. As well as tea, coffee, and pastries, you'll find kedgeree with smoked haddock, chicken pie, delicious sandwiches and baguettes. Main meals include steak, lamb, chicken or fish dishes.

RESTAURANTS: The Victorian Restaurant is more formal and has a carvery and an à la carte menu. Starters include grilled halloumi, duck and orange pâté, crab and avocado, and soup of the day. Main courses feature steaks and grills, fish dishes, ginger chicken, pork and venison. Round off your meal with a mouth-watering dessert such as triple chocolate Boston custard cake, lemon and lime cheese cake or profiterole mountain. In the basement, Albert's Restaurant specialises in the old English favourite of fish and chips, freshly-cooked to perfection.

OPENING TIMES:

Café Bar:		
All week	12.00am - 5.00pm	
Restaurant:		
All week	12.00am - 2.30pm	
	6.00pm - 9.30pm	

On Sundays the restaurant closes at 9.00pm

DIRECTIONS: Take M4 to J6 then A332. Follow signs to town centre.

£ - £££

DICKENS CONNECTION

My Dear Salmon.
I don't know whether it was because I had caught my wife's cold; or because of my being weak, and having stood too long, finishing Barnaby; but yesterday and the evening before, all manner of queer pains were floating about my illustrious person: now twitching at the calves of my legs-now sticking shadowy pins into the soles of my feet-now entertaining themselves with my knees-now (but not often) shooting through that region which you have made as tender as my heart-and now settling in the small of my back; but particularly favouring the back; and the calves before mentioned.

Extract from letter that Dickens wrote to Frederick Salmon whilst staying at the White Hart Hotel on 7th November 1841. (Ye Harte & Garter was called the White Hart Hotel.)

South West

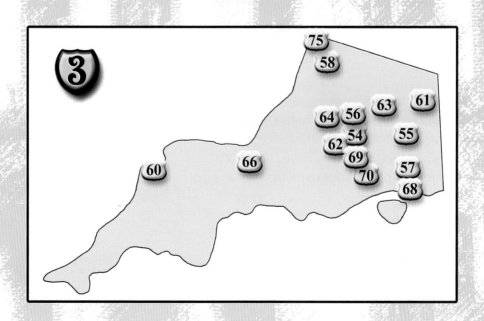

The George Hotel

High Street
Amesbury
Wiltshire
SP4 7ET

Tel : 01980 622 108
Fax : 01980 622 208

Web :
www.chapmansgroup.com

HISTORY: The George, nestling in the town centre of Amesbury on the Salisbury Plain, is just a short distance from Stonehenge. Originally it was the Pilgrims' Hostelry attached to Amesbury Abbey which was founded in AD 900. The hotel has been mentioned in Crown records dating back to the 16th and 17th centuries. Amesbury was on the route of the 'Quicksilver' which was the old London to Exeter mailcoach and was the halfway stop-over for tired travellers to eat and rest and for the horses to be changed. Over the years, the hotel has been host to the rich and famous including Sir Winston Churchill and Field Marshall Montgomery. It was used as the campaign headquarters of General Fairfax during the English Civil War.

BAR: Surrounded by original oak beams and open fires, the bar is the perfect place to relax and enjoy a delicious variety of traditional pub food. Choose from sandwiches and baguettes with various fillings, jacket potatoes, and an assortment of savoury snacks.

RESTAURANT: In the historic setting of the restaurant, the chef takes great pride in the creation of traditional English food with starters such as farmhouse pâté, prawn cocktail, and soup. Main courses include steak pie, or sausages and mash. From the carvery, roasts are served with all the trimmings as well as steaks, chicken, fish and a choice of freshly-prepared salads. If you can find room, try one of the dreamy desserts such as passion cake, banana boat or cheese cake, and hot puds like treacle sponge or jam roly poly.

OPENING TIMES:
Bar/Restaurant:
All Week   12.00am -   9.00pm

DIRECTIONS: A303 to town centre.

DICKENS CONNECTION

"The mistress of the Blue Dragon was in outward appearance just what a landlady should be; broad, buxom, comfortable, and good-looking, with a face of clear red and white, which, by its jovial aspect, at once bore testimony to her hearty participation in the good things of the larder and the cellar, and to their thriving and healthful influences."

"Martin Chuzzlewit"   Book I   Chpt. III
Dickens called the "The George Hotel" the "Blue Dragon"

The Red Lion

London Street
Basingstoke
Hampshire
RG21 7NY

Tel : 01256 328 525
Fax : 01256 844 056
Information Freephone : 0800 435 996

Web : www.zoffanyhotels.co.uk

E-mail : redlion@zoffanyhotels.co.uk

HISTORY: The Red Lion Hotel was originally a 16th century coaching inn, extended over the years but retaining a lot of its original character and charm. Ideally located in the heart of Basingstoke on the old London to Salisbury coaching road, it is a short distance from the local market and shopping centre.

BAR: The spacious bar retains its cosy feel and warm atmosphere. It offers a selection of snacks, such as chunky farmhouse sandwiches served open or as normal. Try the bacon, avocado and tomato or the ocean prawns with Marie Rose sauce -- both delicious! Also available: baguettes, filled jacket potatoes and main courses including locally-made sausages and mash, omelettes, $\frac{1}{2}$lb beef burger topped with salad, cod in light beer batter, chicken and pasta dishes; plus daily specials and desserts from the blackboard.

RESTAURANT: The elegant dining room offers a three-course table d'hôte menu, which is changed regularly and has something to suit all tastes. Choose from starters like steamed mussels in white wine and garlic, coarse country pâté, or melon; follow with steak and kidney pudding or lamb hotpot. If you have a hearty appetite, choose one of the chunky steaks. To complete your meal, try a tempting dessert such as warm bread and marmalade pudding with vanilla custard, apple tart and fresh cream, or chocolate torte with clotted cream. A carvery is available on Sundays.

OPENING TIMES:

Bar:

Monday - Saturday	11.00am -	3.00pm
Sunday	12.00am -	3.00pm
Evenings	5.00pm -	11.00pm
Sunday	7.00pm -	10.30pm

Restaurant:

Monday - Saturday	3.00pm -	6.00pm
Sunday Lunch	12.00am -	2.00pm
Dinner	7.00pm -	9.00pm

DIRECTIONS: Junction 6, M3. Follow signs towards Basingstoke town centre.

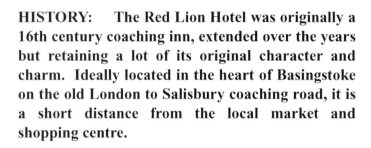

£ - £££

DICKENS CONNECTION

"Away with four fresh horses from the Bald-faced Stag, where toppers congregate about the door admiring; and the last team with traces hanging loose, go roaming off towards the pond, until observed and shouted after by a dozen throats, while volunteering boys pursue them. Now, with a clattering of hoofs and striking out of fiery sparks, across the old stone bridge, and down again into the shadowy road, and through the open gate, and far away, away into the wold".

"Martin Chuzzlewit"   Book II   Chpt. XXXVI
Dickens called the "Red Lion" the "Bald-faced Stag"

The Waggon & Horses

Beckhampton
Nr. Marlborough
Wiltshire
SN8 1QJ

Tel : 01672 539 418

HISTORY: This unique and unusual old waggoners' inn with its thatched roof, mullioned windows and heavy oak doors, stands on the edge of the Marlborough Downs and dates back to 1560. The mellow stone walls were built from smashed stones taken from the nearby Avebury Ring, Europe's largest Neolithic stone circle, dating back to around 2,500 B.C. It was a stopping place for the great eight-wheeled wagons pulled by huge carthorses that trundled along the old Bath Road with horses at the rear to act as a brake. Later, it was an important stop for weary travellers on the London to Bath coaching route. Today, it is a popular haunt with many film and television celebrities.

BAR: The cosy, traditional beamed bar serves a good variety of sandwiches, jacket potatoes, salad platters as well as a selection of toasted sandwiches such as "Horse Bite", which is a toasted club sandwich filled with chicken, lettuce and mayonnaise, bacon and tomato. These are available lunchtimes only, Monday to Saturday.

RESTAURANT: The attractive dining area offers a good selection of main courses with starters such as smoked trout fillet, breaded king prawns, deep-fried Camembert with salad garnish and mango dip. Mains include a delicious beef and Stilton pie, chicken, fish or home-cooked ham plus a substantial steak menu for those of you with hearty appetites. Finish your meal with home-made desserts that include sherry trifle, pineapple upside down cake and Bakewell tart.

OPENING TIMES:

Bar/Restaurant

All week	12.00am - 2.00pm
	7.00pm - 8.30pm

DIRECTIONS:
On main A4 road about halfway between Marlborough and Calne.

DICKENS CONNECTION

"Tom was fond of hot punch - I may venture to say he was very fond of punch - and after he had seen the vixenish mare well fed and well littered down, and had eaten every bit of a nice little hot dinner which the widow tossed up for him with her own hands, he just ordered a tumbler of it, by way of experiment. Now, if there was one thing in the whole range of domestic art, which the widow could manufacture better than another, it was this identical article; and the first tumbler was adapted to Tom Smart's taste with such peculiar nicety, that he ordered a second with the least possible delay."

"Pickwick Papers"   Book I   Chpt. XIV
"The Bagman's Story"

The Red Lion

Chalton
Nr. Horndean
Hampshire
PO8 0BG

Tel : 023 9259 2246

HISTORY: Records show the Red Lion began its life in 1147 as a workshop/residence for the craftsmen constructing St. Michael's Church opposite. By 1460, it had become a hostel for dignitaries from the church and manor, being extended shortly afterwards to help accommodate coachmen on their regular journey from London to Portsmouth. In 1503, the Red Lion was first granted its licence and by the 1700s an additional extension was needed to cater for the large number of people who frequented the inn. With its thatched roof, white daub and wood construction, the Red Lion is one of the oldest and most beautiful public houses in the south of England.

BAR: The ancient oak beams and Inglenook fireplace add to the charm of the cosy and comfortable bar. Dishes to tempt your taste buds include freshly-made sandwiches, with a choice of fillings, baguettes filled with Red Lion steak, bacon lettuce and tomato; coronation chicken, baked jacket potatoes or ploughman's. There is a good variety of home-cooked food; one of the most popular dishes is beefsteak and kidney pie cooked in Gales ale.

RESTAURANT: Built in 1988 with views over-looking the garden, the attractive dining room has an extensive chalked menu-board which is changed frequently. It offers a choice of starters and tempting main courses, with a selection of home-made desserts and speciality ice cream sundaes. The Red Lion has won pub of the year awards, and is recognised in *The Good Beer Guide* for its selection of real ale.

OPENING TIMES:

Bar/Restaurant:

Monday - Saturday	12.00am -	2.00pm
Friday - Saturday	6.30pm -	9.30pm
Sunday	12.00am -	2.30pm

DIRECTIONS: A3 London-Portsmouth Road; about 12 miles from Portsmouth. Signposts to Chalton and Clanfield.

DICKENS CONNECTION

"Why, then I'll tell you what", rejoined the landlord. "There's a gentleman in the parlour that's ordered a hot beef-steak pudding and potatoes, at nine. There's more of it than he can manage, and I have very little doubt that if I ask leave, you can sup with him. I'll do that in a minute." "No, No," said Nicholas, detaining him. "I would rather not I-at least-pshaw! why cannot I speak out? Here; you see that I am travelling in a very humble manner, and have made my way hither on foot."

"Nicholas Nickleby"   Book I   Chpt. XXII

The Queen's Hotel

Reading Tour 1869

Assembly Rooms, Cheltenham.

Messrs. Chappell & Co. beg to announce that they have made arrangements with

MR. CHARLES DICKENS

FOR ONE

FAREWELL READING,

(The last that Mr. Dickens will ever give in Cheltenham)

On FRIDAY EVENING, Jan. 22nd, 1869,

When he will read his

BOOTS AT THE HOLLY TREE INN

SIKES AND NANCY,

(From Oliver Twist) ; and

MRS. GAMP.

It is scarcely necessary for Messrs. Chappell & Co. to add that any announcement made in c... nexion with these Farewell Readings will be strictly adhered to and considered final; and that on no consideration whatever with Mr. Dickens be induced to appoint an extra night in any place in which he shall have been announced to read for the last time.

The Reading will commence at Eight o'c'ock, and be comprised within two hours. The audience is earnestly requested to be seated Ten Minutes before the commencement of the Reading.

Stalls (a limited number only). 10s. 6d. Reserved Seats, 7s. 6d. Second Seats, 4s. Admission, 1s.

Tickets may be obtained of Messrs. FINLAYSON & Co. at their Music Warehouse, 8, Promenade Villas, where the Plan of the Room may be seen and Places secured.

Arrivals

AT THE QUEEN'S HOTEL.—Lady Lopes, Major-Gen. Watkins, Col. and Mrs. Mackenzie, Capt. Dwarris, Capt. Hammond, Capt. and Miss Macdonald, Capt. Stanley, Mr. and Mrs. Pilling, Mr. and Mrs. Pinchard, Mr. and Miss Symons, and Mrs. Wilson ; Messrs. E. Blakeney, Brassey, Bridges, C. Dickens, Mellor, Nickolas, Owen, E. Sarel, Thornton, and Worley.

The Queen's Hotel

The Promenade
Cheltenham
Gloucestershire
GL50 1NN

Tel : 0807 400 1087
Fax : 0124 222 4145

E-mail : queens@heritage-hotels.co.uk

OPENING TIMES:

Bar:
   All week   11.00am - 11.00pm

Restaurant:
   All week   12.30pm - 2.30pm
                      7.00pm - 9.45pm

~~~~~~

HISTORY: The discovery in 1716 of health-giving spring waters in Cheltenham led to a huge expansion in the town. Spas were built to allow fashionable people to take the waters. The inns and lodging houses had difficulty in meeting the demand for accommodation, and when King George III visited with his family, Cheltenham became an even more popular holiday destination which made it necessary to build some proper hotels.

So the story of the Queen's Hotel began. In 1834, a group of entrepreneurial citizens formed a joint Stock Company and decided to build a grand hotel for the many eminent people who wished to visit the town. It was to be 250 feet long, the front and side would be adorned by more than 50 Corinthian columns, and it cost a staggering £45,000 (many millions of pounds today). It was described as one of the most classical and elegant edifices of its kind in Europe, standing in a spectacular position at the top of the tree-lined promenade.

In 1840, the facade was illuminated to celebrate Queen Victoria's wedding. Over the years, many eminent people have stayed at The Queen's including royals, politicians, high-ranking soldiers, writers and musicians. During the Second World War, the hotel was used as a hospital for men returning from Dunkirk, and later as a Services Club for American troops. Cheltenham is one of the most complete Regency towns in the country and has over 2,000 notable listed buildings.

BAR/LOUNGE: The spacious and comfortable lounge offers a very comprehensive choice of snacks and main meals including starters and light bites; try chicken liver and brandy pâté with spicy apple and plum chutney, three egg omelette with a choice of smoked salmon, mushroom or cheese served with a green salad, or a wide range of sandwiches including toasted club sandwiches. Main meals feature grilled Scottish ribeye steak, roasted duck, chicken, fish and pasta dishes. To complete your meal, there's a tempting choice of desserts. Morning coffee is also available and afternoon cream teas, for which the hotel is renowned.

RESTAURANT: The stylish and elegant Napier Restaurant has an innovative à la carte menu with a wide choice of classic and international cuisine with starters such as venison and champagne terrine with hot pepper jelly; sweet pear, rocket, watercress, walnut and Parmesan salad. Main courses include imaginative dishes, beautifully presented, which can be roast rump of lamb on a rosti potato with mint jus; pan-fried breast of Barbary duck, lemon grass and cracked black pepper couscous. Fish, steak, and vegetarian dishes are also offered as well as a choice of yummy desserts such as cappuccino crème brulée, a selection of ice creams in a brandy snap basket, and marmalade bread and butter pudding. The menu is complemented by a good selection of fine wines from around the world.

DIRECTIONS: The hotel is in the town centre opposite the park at the top of the promenade.

The Red Lion Hotel

The Quay
Clovelly
Nr. Bideford
North Devon
EX39 5TF

Tel : 01237 431 237
Fax : 01237 431 044

E-mail :
redlion@clovelly.co.uk

HISTORY: This is a delightful 18th century hostelry, formerly a beer house frequented by local fishermen and villagers. In the residents' lounge, there is a copy of the original 17th century letter from Charles II to Sir John Rous, expressing the King's appreciation of his subjects' loyalty during his exile. The family today still administer the Clovelly estate. The hotel has a superb location by the restored 14th century quay and picturesque harbour. The village of Clovelly is a photographer's paradise. To reach the hotel, you either walk down the steep, cobbled street known as 'Up-Along' or take the official Clovelly Land Rover.

THE SNUG BAR/HARBOUR BAR: Two delightful bars, each with their own character, serve freshly prepared hot and cold snacks.

RESTAURANT: Overlooking the bay, the dining room is the perfect setting in which to enjoy seafood brought fresh from the harbour that morning. There is a variety of delectable dishes -- starters can include fennel and spring onion soup with herb croutons, green-lipped mussels, or crispy duck and orange salad circled by rich plum sauce. Main courses can include freshly-caught Clovelly lobster, a trio of salmon, monkfish and cod presented with roasted garlic and baby onions with a basil sauce, or pan-fried sirloin of beef on a bed of pesto mashed potato with a rich red wine jus. There is a good selection of tempting desserts to follow.

OPENING TIMES:

Bar:
All week   12.00am - 2.30pm
                      6.00pm - 8.30pm
Restaurant:
All week   7.00pm - 10.30pm

DIRECTIONS: A39 from Bideford -- B3237 from Clovelly Cross.

£ - £££

DICKENS CONNECTION

Charles Dickens together with Wilkie Collins visited Clovelly in 1860 to gather material for a story they were jointly writing for the Christmas edition of his magazine 'All the Year Round'. They called the story "Message from the Sea" and Clovelly became Steepways.

~~~~~~~~~~~~~~~~~~~

"Thus replying, and enjoining Tom to give an eye to the shop, Captain Jorgan followed Mrs. Raybrock into the little, low back room, - decorated with divers plants in pots, tea-trays, old china teapots, and punch bowls, - which was at once the private sitting-room of the Raybrock family and the inner cabinet of the post-office of the village of Steepways."

"Christmas Stories"   Book I
Message from the Sea - 1860.

The Red Lion

Henley-on-Thames
Oxfordshire
RG9 2AR

Tel : 01491 572 161
Fax : 01491 410 039

Web :
www.redlionhenley.co.uk

E-mail :
reservations@redlionhenley.co.uk

HISTORY: The Red Lion stands in a prominent position beside the River Thames overlooking the Royal Regatta course. It is believed the hotel was originally built in 1531. The town of Henley has been standing beside the river since long before the Norman Conquest in 1066. Three kings of England have enjoyed the hospitality of the hotel, the earliest was Charles Ist, who stayed in the hotel in 1632 en route from London to Oxford. The original Coat of Arms, painted above the fireplace in one of the rooms, has been preserved and glassed over following its discovery during alterations in 1889. The Duke of Marlborough often stayed at the hotel on his way from Blenheim Palace to London.

BAR: In the traditional warm atmosphere of the Snug Bar there is a selection of hot food -- soup, fish, jacket potatoes, steak and club sandwiches; also available, a selection of freshly-prepared sandwiches, served with a side salad and home-made crisps.

RESTAURANT: Modern and classic dishes from the imaginative menu are served in the delightful, airy restaurant. Starters can include red onion tarte tatin with a pine nut, goats' cheese and poached pear salad or rabbit terrine served with Bramley apple jelly and toasted brioche, Follow with main courses such as fillet of beef with dauphinoise potatoes, wild mushrooms and a herb butter; and monkfish roasted in pancetta. Round off your meal with a sumptuous dessert such as iced Grand Marnier soufflé with orange tuiles and an apricot coulis or hot

chocolate pudding with white chocolate ice cream. The menu is complemented by an extensive wine list.

OPENING TIMES:

All week

Bar/Restaurant	12.30pm - 2.00pm
Tea	3.00pm - 6.00pm
Restaurant	7.00pm - 9.45pm

DIRECTIONS: M4 J9. Take A423 to town centre, next to Henley Bridge.

£ - £££

DICKENS CONNECTION

"He has put up for the night at an Angler's Inn" was the fatigued and hoarse reply. "He goes on, up the river at six in the morning. I have come back for a couple of hours 'rest'."

"Our Mutual Friend"   Book IV   Chpt. 1

The Wheatsheaf

**Lower Woodford
Salisbury
Wiltshire
SP4 6NQ**

Tel : 01722 782 203

HISTORY: The building was originally a farmhouse dating from the 17th century; it has been sympathetically converted into a public house with a delightful interior. The Wheatsheaf stands in a picturesque valley beside the River Avon in the charming hamlet of Lower Woodford, which lies between Salisbury and Amesbury. In the early days, the pub brewed its own beers.

BAR: The open-plan bar offers a large selection of snacks such as ploughman's, filled jacket potatoes and freshly-made sandwiches; choose from thick-cut rustic bread, ciabatta or foccacia. Hot dishes include home-cooked Wiltshire ham with egg and chips, speciality sausages with mustard mash and onion gravy; also pasta dishes or fish coated in beer batter.

RESTAURANT: Your meals are served in the attractive dining area and include a good variety of starters such as home-made soup of the day to garlic king prawns. Main courses can be oriental duck breast with pak choi, shiitake mushrooms and oriental dressing; venison steak, seared salmon fillet or chicken. Sirloin, rump and marinated lamb steaks are served from the grill. All dishes come with potatoes and fresh market vegetables. A tempting choice of home-made desserts include chocolate and orange sponge, apple and blackberry crumble, strawberry cheesecake and banoffee pie.

OPENING TIMES:

Bar/Restaurant

Monday - Saturday	12.00am -	9.00pm
Sunday	12.00am -	8.00pm

DIRECTIONS:
Approximately four miles north of Salisbury turn off A360 at signpost.

DICKENS CONNECTION

"When they were half-way home, and stopped to give the horse some water, Martin (who was very generous with his money) ordered another glass of punch, which they drank between them, and which had not the effect of making them less conversational than before. Their principal topic of discourse was naturally Mr. Pecksniff and his family; of whom, and of the great obligations they had heaped upon him, Tom Pinch, with the tears standing in his eyes, drew such a picture, as would have inclined any one of common feeling almost to revere them."

"Martin Chuzzelwit"   Chpt. V

The Dolphin Inn

**Bartholomew Street
Newbury
Berkshire
RG14 5DT**

Tel : 0163 548 167

HISTORY: The Dolphin Inn (formerly called The George and Pelican) dates back to the 17th century and is a grade II listed building. The inn stands on the Great Western Road and occupies a prominent position at the junction of crossroads leading to Oxford, Bath and London, and was a stopping place for as many as 42 coaches a day. Lord Nelson frequently stayed at the inn on his way to visit his father who lived in Bath. Charles Dickens, first visit to the inn was on the 10th November 1835. He was writing for the *Morning Chronicle* and was on his way to Bristol to report on a dinner given by the people of that city to honour Lord John Russell. Some ten years later, Dickens returned to the inn and it is possible this visit led to his graphic description of an *Old Stage-Coaching House* published in his magazine *All The Year Round* on August 1st 1863. There's little doubt that the town was Newbury and The Dolphin's Head (the name Dickens called the inn) was the old George and Pelican. Over the course of time, the name became The Dolphin Inn.

BAR: The comfortable and attractive bar serves a good selection of snacks including sandwiches, baguettes and jacket potatoes with a choice of fillings.

RESTAURANT: A wide choice of freshly-prepared home-cooked food is available and includes starters such as deep-fried potato skins topped with melted cheese, and pâté with toast. Main courses offer a selection of roasts, fish, steak, sausages and chicken, and a tempting selection of desserts.

OPENING TIMES:

Bar/Restaurant:

All week	12.00am - 3.30pm
	7.00pm - 9.30pm

DIRECTIONS: M4 J13 take A34/A343 to town centre. The inn is really near the Kennet Shopping Centre.

DICKENS CONNECTION

"The sign of the house was the Dolphin's Head. Why only head, I don't know; for the Dolphin's effigy at full length, and upside down - as a dolphin is always bound to be artistically treated, though I suppose he is sometimes right side upward in his natural condition - graced the sign-board. The sign-board chafed its rusty hooks outside the bow-window of my room, and was a shabby work. No visitor could have denied that the Dolphin was dying by inches, but he showed no bright colours. He had once served another master; there was a newer streak of paint below him, displaying with inconsistent freshness the Legend, by J. Mellows."

"The Uncommercial Traveller"   Chpt. XXIV
An Old Stage-coaching House.

Hare & Hounds

**Pickwick
Nr. Corsham
Wiltshire
SN13 0HY**

Tel : 01249 701 106

HISTORY: An historic coaching inn dating from the reign of George III c.1800. It stands on the old coaching road from Oxford to Bath. In 1694, a baby was found abandoned by the side of the road near Pickwick and was taken to Corsham where he was baptised Moses Pickwick: Moses, because he was found, and Pickwick because of the location. In 1782 one of his descendants was born and named Moses Pickwick after him. He became a famous coach proprietor and hotelier and owned The White Hart in the centre of Bath. Dickens named his famous character Mr. Pickwick after him. It is true to say that the real Pickwick wasn't much amused; the reason probably being the type of character Dickens made Mr. Pickwick in his novel. Pickwick blamed Dickens for the decline in his business, but in reality it was the coming of the railways that finished the coaching era. His half-brother, Eleazer Pickwick, was Lord Mayor of Bath in 1826. Moses died in 1869 aged 87 years. Charles Dickens was a frequent visitor to Bath to see his friend Water Savage Landor.

BAR/RESTAURANT: The cosy bar has oak beams, wood panelling and there's a blazing open fire to relax in front of in winter. Hot and cold food is available, and includes a selection of freshly-made sandwiches and baguettes with a choice of fillings, plus jacket potatoes. More substantial dishes may be chicken masala, gammon, curry or steak.

OPENING TIMES:

Bar/Restaurant:

Monday - Friday	12.00am -	2.00pm
	6.00pm -	11.00pm
Saturday	12.00am -	11.00pm
Sunday	12.00am -	10.30pm

Spare a thought as you enter this door. For in this "Historic Inn" situated on the main Road twix Bath and London Charles Dickins stayed whilst writing the "Pickwick Papers."

DIRECTIONS: Take the A4 road to Corsham. Then follow signs to the village.

🚗 ☺ £ - ££

DICKENS CONNECTION

Charles Dickens is believed to have stopped at the pub when visiting Bath.

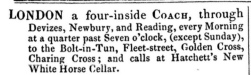

PUBLIC CARRIAGES

WHICH SET OUT FROM THE

WHITE-HART INN,

BATH.

LONDON a four-inside COACH, through Devizes, Newbury, and Reading, every Morning at a quarter past Seven o'clock, (except Sunday), to the Bolt-in-Tun, Fleet-street, Golden Cross, Charing Cross; and calls at Hatchett's New White Horse Cellar.

———— REGULATOR a four-inside COACH, through Devizes, Marlborough, Newbury, and Reading, every Afternoon at half-past Five o'clock, to the Golden Cross, Charing Cross, Bolt-in-Tun, Fleet-street, and Cross Keys, Wood-street, Cheapside.

OXFORD four-inside COACH, through Tetbury, Cirencester, Fairford, Lechlade, and Farringdon, every Morning at Nine o'clock, (except Sunday).

SOUTHAMPTON ROCKET a four-inside COACH, through Warminster, Salisbury, and Romsey, at Eight, (except Sunday)

PORTSMOUTH CELERITY a four-inside COACH, through Warminster, Salisbury, Romsey, Southampton, Fareham and Cosham, every Morning at half-past Eight, (except Sunday,) without changing Coaches.

BRIGHTON a four-inside COACH, in Two days, through Warminster, Salisbury, Romsey, Southampton, Chichester, Arundel, Worthing, and Shoreham, every Morning at Eight o'clock, (except Sunday). Sleeps at Southampton, and arrives early the following afternoon.

*** The above Coaches are in direct communication with the Packets from Southampton to Havre-de-Grace, and Caen, in Normandy.

WEYMOUTH JOHN BULL a four-inside COACH, through Frome, Bruton, Wincanton, Sherborne, and Dorchester, Tuesday, Thursday, and Saturday Mornings, at half-past Eight.

*** The above Coach is in direct communication with the Packets from Weymouth to Jersey & Guernsey.

BIRMINGHAM MERCURY a four-inside COACH, through Rodborough, Gloucester, Tewkesbury, Worcester, and Broomsgrove, every Morning at Eight (except Sunday).

BIRMINGHAM MAIL every evening at half-past four.

LIVERPOOL a four-inside COACH, through Birmingham, every Morning at Eight (except Sunday).

MANCHESTER a four-inside COACH, through Birmingham, every Morning at Eight, (except Sunday).

NOTTINGHAM a four-inside COACH through Birmingham, every Morning at Eight (except Sunday).

GLOUCESTER a four-inside COACH, every Morning at Eight and Ten o'clock, (except Sunday.)

WORCESTER a four-inside COACH every Morning at Eight o'clock, (except Sunday).

SHREWSBURY and **HOLYHEAD** a four-inside COACH, through Gloucester, Cheltenham, Worcester, Kidderminster, Bridgnorth, and Much Wenlock, every Morning at Ten o'clock (except Sunday); sleeps at Cheltenham, and Shrewsbury.—From whence the PRINCE OF WALES, Light Post COACH, leaves every morning at Six, and arrives at the Hibernia Hotel, Holyhead, at 8 the same Evening.

CHELTENHAM a four-inside COACH, through Rodborough, Cain-Cross, and Gloucester, every Morning at Ten o'clock, (except Sunday).

HEREFORD a four-inside COACH, every Morning (except Sunday).

EXETER a four-inside COACH, through Wells, Bridgwater, Taunton, and Collumpton, every Morning, (except Sunday), at half-past 7.

PLYMOUTH a four-inside COACH, through Wells, Bridgwater, Taunton, Collumpton, and Exeter, every Morning (except Sunday) at half-past Seven.

POOLE WELLINGTON, a four-inside COACH, every Monday, Wednesday, and Friday Morning at Nine o'clock, through Frome, Bradley, Stourhead, Bourton, Gillingham, Shaftesbury, Blandford, and Wimborne, to the Antelope Inn, Poole, and returns the following Morning.

CLIFTON a four-inside COACH, every Morning at 10 o'clock, (except Sunday).

———— a four-inside COACH, every Afternoon, at 3 and 4 (except Sunday).

BRISTOL COACHES, every Morning at 7 and 8.
Ditto at 10, 11, and 12 (except Sunday.)
Every Afternoon at 1.
Ditto at 2, and 3, (except Sunday, 4) half-past 4.
Ditto 5 and at 6.
Ditto at 7 (except Sunday.)
Ditto every evening at 8.

FROME every morning at half-past 8, ditto every evening (except Sunday) at a quarter past 6 o'clock.

SALISBURY, every Morning (except Sunday) at 8 and half-past 8.

WESTON SUPER MARE, every morning, at 7, during the Summer season.

Performed by **M. PICKWICK, & Co.**

Passengers and Parcels forwarded, with the greatest dispatch, from this Office, to all parts of the Kingdom.

Black Carriages and Horses for Funerals.

Charles Dickens used the name of the Bath coach proprietor Moses Pickwick for his famous novel *"Pickwick Papers"*.

The Castle Hotel

The Castle Hotel

Castle Green
Taunton
Somerset
TA1 1NF

Tel : 01823 272 671
Fax : 01823 336 066

Web : www.the-castle-hotel.com
E-mail : reception@the-castle-hotel.com

HISTORY: A hotel of distinction, built on the historic site of Taunton Castle. The first castle was built in the 8th century by the King of Wessex, and is England's oldest recorded fortress. In 1001 the castle and town were burnt to the ground by the Danes, but 50 years later, both were flourishing again and before 1066 a third castle was in existence. In 1495, Perkin Warbeck, pretending to be the Duke of York (one of the princes murdered in the Tower), arrived at Taunton and proclaimed himself Richard IV. However, Henry VII recaptured the castle and Warbeck was tried for treason. The Duke of Monmouth, illegitimate son of Charles II, tried to overthrow his uncle James II, at the Battle of Sedgemoor in 1685. Monmouth's army was defeated and his troops were taken to Taunton Castle and imprisoned there before being tried in the castle's Great Hall by the notorious Judge Jeffries at one of his "Bloody Assizes", where he sentenced 158 prisoners to be hung, drawn and quartered. Later on, the castle fell into disuse and was dismantled, part of it being used as a hostel, but it has been an hotel for the past 300 years, with much of the medieval interior being incorporated into the present structure. The archway, circa 1300, under the south wing of the hotel and over the old London to Plymouth coaching road, was originally the old eastern gate of the castle's outer bailey. Today, the front of the building is covered by a magnificent 150 year-old wisteria. Many famous people have patronised the hotel including Queen Victoria and her mother the Duchess of Kent, King Edward VII, King Edward VIII, the Duke of Wellington, Samuel Taylor Coleridge, Benjamin Disraeli, Queen Elizabeth the Queen Mother, Princess Margaret, Princess Alexandra and the present Duchess of Kent.

RESTAURANT: In the elegant and formal restaurant, you can enjoy modern British and cosmopolitan cuisine with both table d'hôte and à la carte menus with many delightful creations on offer. Starters can be langoustine soup, terrine of dried fruits with seared foie gras and hazelnut dressing, scrambled duck egg with smoked eel and spiced oil, followed by mains like fillet of turbot with buttered cabbage, bacon and cheese potato cake; sirloin of beef with greens and mash, or roe deer with baked squash, creamed leeks, girolles and bacon. Mouth-watering desserts will be hard to resist and may be apricot mousse with praline and apricot ice cream, white chocolate macadamia with a yoghurt ice cream, or golden raisin soufflé with mead jelly. A selection of the finest British cheese is also offered. Most of the hotel's suppliers are based in the West Country and are chosen for their consistent quality and the freshness of their produce.

OPENING TIMES:
Restaurant: All week 12.30pm - 2.00pm
                         7.00pm - 9.30pm

DIRECTIONS:
M5 J25 About two miles to town centre.

🚗 ⊗ 🚂 💳 🖦 £££+

The George

84 - 85 Queen Street
Portsmouth
Hampshire
PO1 3HU

Tel : 02392 872 000

HISTORY: In the Portsmouth Directory of 1784, The George appears as a tavern and claims to be the last surviving 18th century public house in Portsmouth. At one time it was the stopping place for coaches leaving Portsmouth travelling to London. The name was changed in 1905 to the King George, but during restoration it was decided to revert to the original name. Situated close to the dockyard gates, the inn has seen much of the comings and goings of maritime life and has many tales to tell. Between the two original buildings there was a courtyard with a well, which could be shared by the two properties. At the end of the 19th century, the well was covered over but not filled in. However, during further restoration work the two buildings were integrated into one, and the well is now a feature in the bar. The bottom of the well is 40 feet deep with the water level 12 feet from the surface. Two walls were also taken out of the lower level when extending the cellar and replaced by large oak beams;one timber bears the name 'Ariadne' which was carved on one side by the shipwright. Oak was readily available from the last of the ships' "wooden walls" being broken up in the dockyard. The carved rope timber was one of many that were once gilded and used on the upper deck of the Royal Yacht, Victoria and Albert III.

BAR: The old oak beams and the many pictures creates a nostalgic atmosphere where the feeling of the 18th century can be captured and enjoyed. Food available includes bar snacks such as sandwiches, baguettes and jacket potatoes.

RESTAURANT: The attractive wood-panelled dining room offers traditional English home-cooked food, which is freshly-prepared using local produce. Opt for fish and chips, steak and ale pie, or ham and chicken, with desserts such as steamed puddings and ice creams. On Sundays, there is a choice of roasts.

OPENING TIMES:

Bar/Restaurant:

Monday - Saturday	12.00am	-	2.30pm
	6.00pm	-	9.00pm
Sunday	12.00am	-	2.30pm

<u>**No food served Sunday evening.**</u>

DIRECTIONS:
Follow signs to the Historic Dockyard. The George is near the Victory gate.

£ - ££

DICKENS CONNECTION

Dickens' family local whilst living at nearby Hawke Street.

The Red Lion

Milford Street
Salisbury
Wiltshire
SP1 2AN

Tel : 01722 32 33 34
Fax : 01722 32 57 56

Web :
www.the-redlion.co.uk

E-mail :
reception@the-redlion.co.uk

HISTORY: The Red Lion is possibly the longest running purpose-built hotel in England. It was built over 750 years ago to house the many draughtsmen working on the nearby cathedral. During recent times, many modern facilities have been added to the hotel without spoiling its unique character and atmosphere. There is a fine collection of antiques throughout the hotel -- especially the many clocks -- including 'Parliament Clocks' and, in particular, the 'Skeleton and Organ Clock' in the reception hall. In fine weather, you can dine al fresco in the magnificent vine-covered courtyard.

BAR: In the comfortable bar, there is a large selection of sandwiches and baguettes, as well as an extensive menu of interesting hot and cold dishes.

RESTAURANT: The restaurant has a delightful ambience with its fine china collection and "wattle and daub" walls dating back to the 13th century. There is an extensive choice on the menu of both English and Continental cuisine, with starters such as baked tomatoes and melted mozzarella or quenelles of prawn and chive mousse, followed by braised lamb shank, grilled duck breast, poached salmon and seabass, plus pasta dishes. Choux swan chantilly, lemon mousse or crème brúlée, are some of the tempting desserts available. Food is also served on Sundays, which includes a choice of roasts, and there is a comprehensive wine list to savour.

OPENING TIMES:

Monday - Saturday

Bar	12.00am -	2.00pm
	6.30pm -	9.30pm
Restaurant	7.00pm -	9.00pm

Sunday

Bar	12.30pm -	2.00pm
Restaurant	12.00am -	2.00pm
	7.00pm -	9.00pm

DIRECTIONS:
Enter Salisbury via Exeter Street; continue into Catherine Street and turn right into Milford Street.

Ⓟ 🚭 ⊜ ♿ 🪑 💳 VISA 📷 £ - £££

DICKENS CONNECTION

"He had a little table drawn out close to the fire, and fell to work upon a well-cooked steak and smoking hot potatoes, with a strong appreciation of their excellence, and a very keen sense of enjoyment, beside him, too, there stood a jug of the most stupendous Wiltshire beer".

"Martin Chuzzelwit"   Book I   Chpt. V

Mrs Charles Dickens
1, Devonshire Terrace
York Gate
Regents Park
London.

White Hart
Salisbury

Monday Twenty Sixth March 1848

My Dearest Kate,

I have just time to say that we have been out on the Plain on horseback all day - the greater part of it at full gallop. We were excellently mounted; and though we got wet through at starting, the weather cleared after the first two or three hours, and it became a most glorious expedition. We have come back (to a very fair Inn), and changed, and are now waiting for dinner.

There is a sofa in the room, on which, Forster is, of course. lying stretched at full length.

We talk of getting some conveyance to Marlborough tomorrow (30 miles from here) to see some more Druidical remains, and then coming home by the Great Western Railway. But none of our arrangements will interfere with my return sometime tomorrow evening or night.

Best love to the darlings and Grorgy. I hope to find your throat quite well.

Here's the dinner!

Ever affectionately

CD.

Forster sends kind loves.

A copy of a letter written by Charles Dickens to his wife Kate whilst staying at the White Hart - Salisbury.

The White Hart

St. John Street
Salisbury
Wiltshire
SP1 2SD

Tel : 0870 4008 125
Fax : 0172 2412 761

E-mail :
events.whitehartsalisbury@
macdonald-hotels.co.uk

HISTORY: The White Hart was first mentioned in 1618 when it was visited by Sir Walter Raleigh after his failed voyage to Guyana. With its sweeping facade and pillared portico, this elegant hotel stands in the shadow of the famous cathedral. Prior to the present structure being built, the hotel was a coaching inn on the Bristol to Southampton road. In the winter months, huge log fires burn in open fireplaces in the comfortable lounges and, during the summertime, the courtyard is a riot of colour with flowering displays.

THE SPIRES BAR: The comfortable and spacious bar offers a very large selection of food, ranging from sandwiches served with kettle crisps and side salad, filled baked potatoes, specialities of the week such as hot filled baguettes, pasta and fish dishes, to main meals and a good selection of desserts including profiteroles, cheesecake or chef's hot dessert of the day.

THE SQUIRES RESTAURANT: This elegant restaurant offers an imaginative à la carte menu, which may include grilled trout on a chive mash with a caviar cream, fillet of beef on rosti potato with shallot mousse and roasted root vegetables as well as a four-course table d'hôte menu, with delicious starters and desserts. A two or three course table d'hôte menu is served at lunchtime with a good choice of dishes. The wine list includes special wines from Wiltshire.

OPENING TIMES:
  All week
Bar:

Lunch	12.30pm -	2.00pm
Dinner	7.00pm -	9.30pm

Restaurant:

Lunch	12.30pm -	2.00pm
Dinner	7.00pm -	9.30pm

DIRECTIONS: Follow ring road to its southernmost point and then turn into Exeter Street towards the City centre. The hotel is on right-hand side.

 **£ - £££**

DICKENS CONNECTION

"Nobody ever dreamed such soup as was put upon the table directly afterwards; or such fish; or such side dishes; or such a top and bottom; or such a course of birds and sweets; or in short anything approaching the reality of that entertainment at ten-and-sixpence a head, exclusive of wines. As to them, the man who can dream such iced champagne, such claret, port, or sherry, had better go to bed and stop there."

"Martin Chuzzelwit"   Book I   Chpt. XII

GENERAL POST-OFFICE.

Duke of MANCHESTER, His Majesty's Postmaster-General.

London, Exeter and *Devonport* TIME BILL.

Contractors' Names.	Number of Passengers In.	Out.	M.	F.	Time allowed. H. M.		
						Dispatched from the General Post-Office, the of 182 , at *Eight P.M.* {With a Time-Piece safe No. to	
						Coach No. sent out	
						Arrived at the *Gloucester* Coffee-House, at 8 · 20	
Fagg			14 ..6	1	33	Arrived at *Hounslow Heath*, at 9 · 33	
			6 ...2		38	Arrived at *Egham*, at 10 · 11	
			8 ..2		49	Arrived at *Bagshot*, at 11 5	
			10 ..1	1	1	Arrived at *Hartley Row*, at 12 · 1	
			9 ..		54	Arrived at *Basingstoke*, at 12 · 55	
King			7 ..6		47	Arrived at *Overton*, at 1 · 42	
Luscombe			17 ..2	1	45	Arrived at *Wallop*, at 3 · 27	
Harrington			1 ..0	1	6	Arrived at *Salisbury*, at 4 · 33	
			12 ..3	1	15	Arrived at *London Elm*, at 5 · 48	
Gerrard			8 ..		50	Arrived at *Shaftesbury*, at 6 · 38	
Shrimpton & Massey			9 ..5	1	3	Arrived at *Henstridge Ash*, at 7 · 41	
Whitmash			11 ..4	1	15	Arrived thro' *Sherborne*, at *Yeovil*, at 8 · 56 by Time-Piece at by Clock {Delivered the Time-Piece safe No. to	
						Coach No. gone forward	
					30	*Thirty Minutes allowed.*	
Whitmash			9 ...7	1		Arrived at *Crewkerne*, at 10 · 26	
			7 ..7		50	Arrived at *Chard*, at 11 · 16	
Jeffery			5 ...5		40	Arrived at *Yarcombe*, at 11 · 56	
Webber			7 ..5		50	Arrived at *Honiton*, at 12 · 46	
Clench			16 ...3	1	38	Arrived at *Exeter*, at 2 · 24	
					30	*Thirty Minutes allowed.*	
			10 ..7	1	10	Arrived at *Chudleigh*, at 4 - 4	
Weston			9 ..3		55	Arrived at *Ashburton*, at 4 59	
Barron & Stevenet			13 ..	1	18	Arrived at *Ivy Bridge*, at 6 · 17	
Elliott			13 ..	1	25	Arrived at the Post-Office, *Devonport*, the of 182 , at 7 · 42 *P.M.* by Time-Piece at by Clock	
	218 ..6	23					
						Coach No. arrived {Delivered the Time-Piece safe No. to	

THE *Time of working each Stage is to be reckoned from the Coach's Arrival ; and as any Time lost, is to be recovered in the course of the Stage, it is the Coachman's Duty to be as expeditious as possible, and to report the Horse-keepers if they are not always ready when the Coach arrives, and active in getting it off. The Guard is to give his best assistance in changing, whenever his Official Duties do not prevent it.*

September, 1827.——200.

By Command of the Postmaster-General,

CHARLES JOHNSON,
Surveyor and Superintendent.

THE WAY THINGS WERE...

The coming of the Industrial Revolution brought to Great Britain a new system of travel -- rail. Prior to the railways, people travelled around by stage coach. The standard of inns, accommodation and food varied considerably. Charles Dickens, as a young Parliamentary reporter having to travel around the country must have observed all these conditions and used them to his advantage in his later books.
Its ironic that Charles Dickens an enthusiast of new technology and the coming of the railways, was involved in the 1865 Staplehurst train crash that nearly killed him. Thereafter, he was a nervous and reluctant rail traveller for the remainder of his life.

THE PORTSMOUTH COACH.
Sold by C. Sheppard, St Peters Hill, Doctors Commons.

Travel.

In the early coaching days, fresh horses were harnessed to the coach only when the passengers stopped for their dinner, and each team was fed and rested at night; later, when coach travel had become a fast means of communication, the horses were changed far more frequently at short stages all along the road.

The travellers on the coaches were also fed and rested at the inns along the road, spending the night in them and starting off again early the next morning. They probably fared less well than the horses, for the inns varied enormously. Accommodation in some of them was not much above the level of stables. Beds, if they existed, were often verminous and had to be shared with strangers. Travellers who could not find a bed or afford a big enough tip to the landlord, slept on the floor; or, with their limbs already aching from the cruel jolting of the coach, they dozed upright in a chair. No one, fortunately, thought much about washing; a nip of brandy was more comforting than a basin of water and brandy was only 4d a glass. It loosened the tongue and revived the spirits of the more timid travellers.

After sitting all day cooped up in the coach, they liked each other rather better after supper than before. If the food was edible and the landlord obliging, they could count themselves lucky; if neither came up to their expectations, there was nothing much they could do about it except grumble among themselves when they got back into the coach at dawn the next morning.

FOOD

Beef and mutton were the staple dishes, whether in large joints or boiled, or cut into rump steaks and juicy chops. Plenty of poultry and game also appeared on the dining table; peacocks, swans and goose at the larger inns, ducks, capons, woodcock, wheatears, larks and even swallows in the summer; and of all nations and countries, England had always been 'the best served of fish, not only of all manner of sea-fish, but also of fresh-water fish and of all manner of sorts of salt-fish'.

There were a dozen ways of cooking eels; spitchcocked, smoked, water-souche, stewed, fried, boiled and baked among them; and since perishable foods could not be quickly and easily transported over the bad roads, each district had its own speciality, giving the traveller a wonderful variety of choice as he journeyed through the country.

Cambridge was famous for its brawn, Newbury for its crayfish, Kent for its huffkins and Melton Mowbray for its pies. There were ducks and apple sauce at Aylesbury, pink lobsters and crabs at Morecambe, venison pies and pasties in Chester, pigeons and pork in Birmingham and ham at York.

Cheddar cheese, Wensleydale, Double Gloucester and Stilton could only be found where they belonged, but gooseberry-pie, gooseberry fool and plum pudding appeared almost everywhere.

At Grantham special cakes were made there called Grantham Whetstones, and travellers relished the famous cakes of Shrewsbury and Banbury and the buns in Bath. England was a paradise for the gourmet and her cooks had never been better.

No one drank water -- it was hard to obtain and often unwholesome. Men, women and children drank ale instead and thrived on it.

Royal Hop Pole Hotel

**Church Street
Tewkesbury
Gloucestershire
GL20 5RT**

Tel : 01684 293 236
Fax : 01684 296 680

Web :
www.regalhotels.co.uk/royalhoppole

HISTORY: Set in a medieval street in the town centre, the charming, half-timbered Royal Hop Pole dates back to the 15th century. The outstanding feature of the front of the Hop Pole is a model of the Royal arms on top of the portico. Many changes have taken place on the building over the years. In the 18th century, the portico on the Georgian frontage was non-existent, and in its place stood a large double-gated entrance to the yard and stables at the rear. In 1914, the building was re-designed and became the basis of the present day Hop Pole.

BAR: There is an excellent choice including toasted teacakes, pastries and sandwiches; light bites such as cold poached salmon with salad and new potatoes, Indian vegetable tikka wrap, or pasta; chef's hot pie of the day, chicken Kiev or roast of the day served from the carvery. Side orders include potato wedges, salad, garlic bread and chips.

RESTAURANT: In the charming panelled dining room, the à la carte menu offers a good choice of modern and traditional food prepared from fresh local produce such as pan-fried breast of duck in kumquat and Cointreau sauce, game casserole, or braised shank of lamb. Steak, chicken and fish dishes are available from the grill. A good selection of imaginative starters and desserts will tempt your taste buds. There is a four-course table d'hôte Sunday lunch menu.

OPENING TIMES:

Bar:

All week	12.00am -	2.00pm
	6.00pm -	9.00pm

Restaurant:

Sunday - Thursday	7.00pm -	9.30pm
Friday - Saturday	7.00pm -	10.00pm

DIRECTIONS: Exit M5 J9 and follow signs to Tewkesbury Abbey. At the War Memorial Cross, go straight over, and the hotel is on the right.

£ - £££

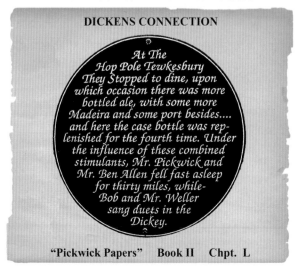

DICKENS CONNECTION

At The Hop Pole Tewkesbury They Stopped to dine, upon which occasion there was more bottled ale, with some more Madeira and some port besides.... and here the case bottle was replenished for the fourth time. Under the influence of these combined stimulants, Mr. Pickwick and Mr. Ben Allen fell fast asleep for thirty miles, while Bob and Mr. Weller sang duets in the Dickey.

"Pickwick Papers"   Book II   Chpt. L

South East & East Anglia

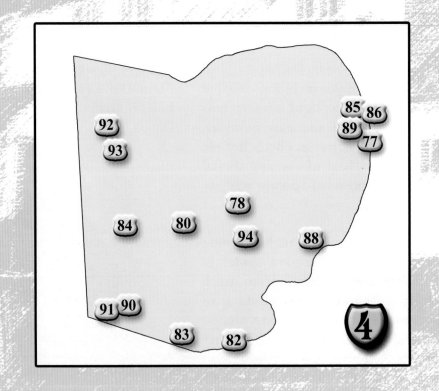

The Plough Inn

Market Lane
Blundeston
Lowestoft
Suffolk
NR32 5AN

Tel : 01502 730 261

Web : www.blundeston.org.uk

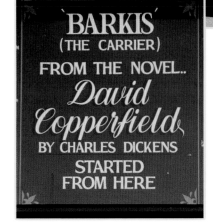

HISTORY: This attractive old inn was built in 1701, in the reign of King William III. Whilst staying at nearby Somerleyton Hall, Charles Dickens came across Blunderston on one of his epic walks. This became Blunderstone, the birthplace of David Copperfield in the novel of the same name. Dickens calls Blunderston Rectory "The Rookery."

BAR: The Barkis Bar has the atmosphere of a traditional inn with its low beams and open fires, where you can enjoy a good selection of bar food such as soup, filled baguettes and sandwiches, jacket potatoes, tuna bake, ploughman's, salad, and breaded scampi.

RESTAURANT: The Copperfield Restaurant offers mainly traditional English dishes which are served with chips, jacket or new potatoes and salad, and includes a selection of starters. There's a good choice of hand-made cold desserts as well as delicious hot puddings, which are changed regularly, plus a selection of ice cream sundaes. All meals are cooked to order from fresh ingredients.

OPENING TIMES:

Bar/Restaurant:	12.00am -	2.30pm
All week	6.30pm -	9.30pm

DIRECTIONS:
A12 between Lowestoft and Great Yarmouth approximately one mile off main road.

£ - ££

DICKENS CONNECTION

The carrier's horse was the laziest horse in the world, I should hope, and shuffled along, with his head down, as if he liked to keep people waiting to whom the packages were directed. I fancied, indeed, that he sometimes chuckled audibly over this reflection, but the carrier said he was only troubled with a cough. The carrier had a way of keeping his head down, like his horse, and of drooping sleepily forward as he drove, with one of his arms on each of his knees. I say "drove," but it struck me that the cart would have gone to Yarmouth quite as well without him, for the horse did all that; and as to conversation, he had no idea of it but whistling. Peggotty had a basket of refreshments on her knee, which would have lasted us out handsomely, if we had been going to London by some conveyance. We ate a good deal, and slept a good deal. Peggotty always went to sleep with her chin upon the handle of the basket, her hold of which never relaxed; and I could not have believed unless I had heard her do it, that one defenceless woman could have snored so much.

"David Copperfield"   Book I   Chpt. III

Angel Hotel
Bury St Edmunds

Wednesday Thirtieth October 1861

My Dearest Georgy

I have just now received your welcome letter, and I hasten to report (having very little time) that we had a splendid Hall last night, and that I think Nickleby tops all the Readings! Somehow it seems to have got in it, by accident, exactly the qualities best suited to the purpose; and it went last night, not only with roars, but with a general hilarity and pleasure that I have never seen surpassed.

We are full here for tonight.

Fancy this:-Last night at about 6, who should walk in but Elwin! He was exactly in his usual state, only more demonstrative than ever, and had been driven in by some neighbours who were coming to the Reading. I had tea up for him, and he went down at 7 with me to the dismal den where I dressed, and sat by the fire while I dressed, and was childishly happy in that great privilege. During the Reading, he sat on a corner of the platform, and roared incessantly. He never said one word about having had any letter from Mary, and I really think his wife must have intercepted those dangerous epistles. He brought in a lady and gentleman to introduce while I was undressing, and went away in a perfect and absolute rapture.

All right as to Barber and the workmen. More workmen are certainly wanted, and can certainly be got.

with best love
Ever My Dearest Georgy   Your most affectionate
CD.

The Athenaeum on the left, is where Charles Dickens gave his Readings, whilst staying at The Angel.

The Angel Hotel

**Angel Hill
Bury St. Edmunds
Suffolk
IP33 1LT**

Tel : 01284 753 926
Fax : 01284 750 092

Web :
www.theangel.co.uk
E-mail :
sales@theangel.co.uk

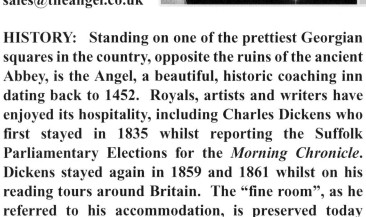

HISTORY: Standing on one of the prettiest Georgian squares in the country, opposite the ruins of the ancient Abbey, is the Angel, a beautiful, historic coaching inn dating back to 1452. Royals, artists and writers have enjoyed its hospitality, including Charles Dickens who first stayed in 1835 whilst reporting the Suffolk Parliamentary Elections for the *Morning Chronicle*. Dickens stayed again in 1859 and 1861 whilst on his reading tours around Britain. The "fine room", as he referred to his accommodation, is preserved today exactly as it was more than 100 years ago.

BAR/LOUNGE: The open fire in the comfortable and spacious lounge creates a warm relaxed atmosphere where morning coffee and traditional afternoon tea is served. At lunchtime and in the evenings, snacks and light meals such as soup of the day, sandwiches and hot bar snacks are also available. For something a little stronger, Suffolk beers, wines and cocktails are served from the Pickwick Bar.

RESTAURANT: There are two restaurants. The Vaults is more informal and is located in the 12th century undercroft -- reputed to be part of the ancient abbey. It serves a good choice of brasserie-style food, and many dishes have a Mediterranean or oriental flavour. Start with courgette and lemon grass soup, followed by seafood risotto or sweet and sour pork with pak choi and noodles. Typical puddings include tiramisu or crème caramel. For a special occasion, head for the grandeur of The Abbeygate restaurant with its royal blue and gold décor and silver service. The chef uses seasonal and local produce where

possible, such as venison from the Denham Estate. Dishes can include warm crab tart on a Noilly Prat cream sauce or salad of game and quails' eggs; main courses receive great attention to detail, featuring staples such as fillet of beef, as well as more imaginative combinations -- lamb with a vegetable gateaux or spicy loin of monkfish with a king prawn samosa. Round off the meal with treats like tarte tatin or berry pancakes, cheeses, beverages, and home-made petit-fours.

OPENING TIMES: All week

Lounge Bar:	11.00am - 3.00pm
	6.00pm - 10.00pm
Abbeygate Restaurant:	12.00am - 2.00pm
	7.00pm - 9.00pm
The Vaults Restaurant:	
Tuesday - Saturday	7.00pm - 9.00pm

DIRECTIONS: Follow signs for cathedral and the historic area.

£ - £££

DICKENS CONNECTION

"The coach rattled through the well-paved streets of a handsome little town, of thriving and cleanly appearance, and stopped before a large inn situated in a wide open street, nearly facing the old abbey. "And this," said Mr. Pickwick, looking up, "is the Angel! We alight here, Sam."

"Pickwick Papers"   Book I   Chpt. XVI

79

DICKENS CONNECTION

My Dearest Georgy,

I write (agreeable to my promise) with all possible dispatch, to let you know the Oxford Train. We start, by the Great Western Railway at 2 o'clock on Monday.

Arthur is at the Agent's and I don't know how we stand here as to the Let. Pretty tolerably, I suppose, But I don't very much like the look of the place. It seems what Plorn would call "ortily" dull.

With loves to the dear girls and to the Noble P.

Ever affecy.

CD.

Letter written to Miss Georgina Hogarth by Charles Dickens on Monday 17th October 1859 whilst staying at the Eagle Hotel, Cambridge.

The Eagle

**Benet Street
Cambridge
Cambridgeshire
CB2 3QN**

Tel : 01223 505 020
Fax : 01223 506 455

HISTORY: The Eagle is an historic gem. A tavern is known to have existed on the site prior to 1353. In 1525, the land was bequeathed to neighbouring Corpus Christi College which has remained the freeholder to the present day. The core of the building dates back to shortly after 1600, and wall decorations thought to date back to this period can be seen in the middle bar. In the early 1800s during the golden age of coaching, the Eagle was an important national staging post, and extensive redevelopment took place to the rear. The arrival of the railways in the 1840s led to a period of decline and the Eagle was divided into a hotel in the front and a tavern at the rear. In 1988, major restoration work was carried out and the pub reopened in 1992.

BARS: There are five comfortable bar areas. The Air Force bar ceiling is of special interest. During the Second World War, the Eagle was a popular meeting place with both English and American airmen, who decorated the ceiling with their signatures and squadron numbers using candlewax and lipstick.

A wide range of hot food is available starting with lighter bites such as hot steak or chicken baguettes, salmon fish cakes or pâté. Main courses may include jumbo battered cod, barbecue ribs, vegetable tikka, pasta dishes, and grilled rump and sirloin steaks. A selection of delectable desserts can be found chalked on the blackboard.

OPENING TIMES:

Lunch:
  All week   12.00am -   2.30pm

Evening Meal:
  Monday - Thursday   5.00pm - 8.45pm
  Friday   5.00pm - 8.00pm

<u>Saturday and Sunday -- no evening meals.</u>

DIRECTIONS:
The Eagle is near King's College Chapel and Corpus Christi College. From M11 there is a park and ride system to the town centre.

£ - ££

DICKENS CONNECTION

Charles Dickens stayed at The Eagle on 17th October 1859, whilst on a Reading tour.

**Haven Road
Canvey Island
Essex
SS8 0NR**

Tel : 01268 660 021

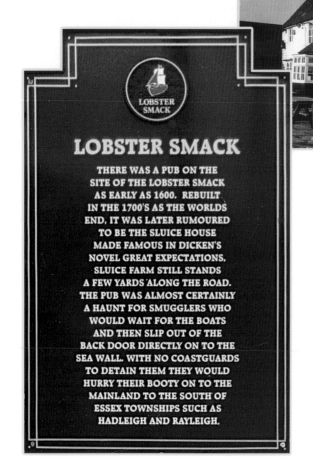

LOBSTER SMACK

THERE WAS A PUB ON THE
SITE OF THE LOBSTER SMACK
AS EARLY AS 1600. REBUILT
IN THE 1700'S AS THE WORLDS
END, IT WAS LATER RUMOURED
TO BE THE SLUICE HOUSE
MADE FAMOUS IN DICKEN'S
NOVEL GREAT EXPECTATIONS.
SLUICE FARM STILL STANDS
A FEW YARDS ALONG THE ROAD.
THE PUB WAS ALMOST CERTAINLY
A HAUNT FOR SMUGGLERS WHO
WOULD WAIT FOR THE BOATS
AND THEN SLIP OUT OF THE
BACK DOOR DIRECTLY ON TO THE
SEA WALL. WITH NO COASTGUARDS
TO DETAIN THEM THEY WOULD
HURRY THEIR BOOTY ON TO THE
MAINLAND TO THE SOUTH OF
ESSEX TOWNSHIPS SUCH AS
HADLEIGH AND RAYLEIGH.

OPENING TIMES:

Bar/Restaurant:

Monday - Saturday	12.00am -	3.00pm
	6.00pm -	9.30pm
Sunday	12.00am -	8.30pm

DIRECTIONS: A130 to Canvey Island.

DICKENS CONNECTION

"Leaving the rest in the boat, I stepped ashore, and found the light to be in the window of a public-house. It was a dirty place enough, and I dare say not unknown to smuggling adventurers; but there was a good fire in the kitchen, and there were eggs and bacon to eat and various liquors to drink. Also, there were two double-bedded rooms – "such as they were," the landlord said. No other company was in the house than the landlord, his wife, and a grizzled male creature, the "Jack" of the little causeway, who was as slimy and smeary as if he had been low water-mark too. With this assistant, I went down to the boat again, and we all came ashore, and brought out the oars, and rudder, and boat-hook, and all else, and hauled her up for the night. We made a very good meal by the kitchen fire, and then apportioned the bedrooms."

"Great Expectations"   Chpt. LIV

BAR: The white weather-boarded old inn, standing close to the river estuary, together with the low beams and log fire inside, creates an atmosphere of bygone days. The cosy bar offers a good choice of hot and cold snacks such as freshly-baked crusty baguettes with hot and cold fillings, jacket potatoes and burgers.

RESTAURANT: A wide range of traditional food is served in the dining area such as sizzling platters of steak, chicken, minted lamb chops or mixed grill. Also available; fish and chips, bangers and mash, Thai red curry, and the manager's specials. Tempting puds to complete your meal include chocolate mallow, baked apple squidgy or strawberry ice cream sundae.

Ye Olde King's Head

**High Street
Chigwell
Essex
IG7 6QA**

Tel :
0208 5002 021

HISTORY: This fine old hostelry dates back to the 15th century and lies in the Roding Valley between the two ancient forests of Epping and Hainault. Records show that the King's Head was serving ale and forest venison to wayfarers of Tudor and Stuart times. The sittings of the Forty Day Courts were held at the inn during the days of Queen Elizabeth and James Ist. These were held to settle disputes connected with forest rights of hunting, lopping and pannage. The great lattice-windowed upper room in which the courts were held is now the dining room. Since Dickens wrote *Barnaby Rudge* in 1840, this fine old room has been known as the Chester Room after Sir John Chester, a character in the book. The theatre at the side was made famous in the 1920s by Bransby Williams with his portrayal of Dickens characters. In the summer of 1996, Marlon Brando visited the King's Head.

BAR: In the traditional warm atmosphere, you can opt for a hearty snack or a light bite such as filled baguette, soft rolls, jacket potatoes, various salads, or more substantial main courses like turkey, ham and mushroom pie, scampi, or battered haddock, all served with potatoes and vegetables. A good choice of desserts is always available, such as chocolate orange marble cake, or apple pie.

RESTAURANT: On the first floor, the dining room with its wood-panelled walls still retains its old world charm and serves mainly favourite English dishes.

There's a starter bar where you can help yourself. Succulent roasts are served from the chef's carvery with a tempting variety of fresh vegetables, sauces and trimmings. Alternatively opt for delicious cobblers, tasty pasta or fish dishes. A large choice of desserts include gooseberry crumble, lemon meringue pie or sticky ginger cake. Finish your meal in style with an exotic liquor coffee.

OPENING TIMES:
Bar:

Monday - Friday	12.00am -	2.00pm
	6.00pm -	9.00pm
Saturday - Sunday	12.00am -	9.00pm

Restaurant:

Monday - Friday	12.00am -	2.00pm
Saturday - Sunday	12.00am -	9.00pm

DIRECTIONS:
Take A12 then A1112 or M11 J5.

DICKENS CONNECTION

"A bit of fish," said John to the cook, "and some lamb chops (breaded, with plenty of ketchup), and a good salad, and a roast spring chicken, with a dish of sausages and mashed potatoes, or something of that sort." Some-thing of that sort! The resources of these inns!"

"Barnaby Rudge"   Book I   Chpt. XIX
Dickens called the "The King's Head" "The Maypole"

The White Horse

**103 Great North Road
Eaton Socon
St. Neots
Cambridgeshire
PE19 3EL**

Tel : 01480 474 453
Fax : 01480 406 650

Mobile : 079 3271 5316

OPENING TIMES:

Monday - Friday	11.00am -	3.00pm
	5.00pm -	11.00pm
Saturday	11.00am -	3.00pm
	5.30pm -	11.00pm
Sunday	12.00am -	3.00pm
	7.00pm -	10.30pm

DIRECTIONS: On A1 Great North Road, take the Black Cat roundabout to Eaton

Ⓟ 🚻 🚭 🚬 ♿ 🎠 💳 VISA £ - £££

HISTORY: The White Horse is a 13th century coaching inn, just off the Great North Road located in the centre of the pretty village of Eaton Socon. The London to York stagecoach used to stop here and rest on its four-day journey. Famous guests included Samuel Pepys and, of course, Charles Dickens. The interior has many interesting features -- a magnificent Inglenook fireplace and cosy antique furnishings are set in a series of well-kept rooms. A glittering mass of horse brasses, bric-à-brac and interesting brass platters add to the general ambience.

BAR/RESTAURANT: The delightful bar and restaurant serves a good selection of tasty and imaginative snacks -- freshly-made sandwiches with a large choice of fillings served with salad garnish, soup of the day, smoked seafood platter, prawn cocktail or Caesar salad. The main menu also gives a large choice of dishes including hickory-smoked barbecue rack of ribs, sweet and sour pork, wholetail Whitby scampi, lasagne, or steak, ale and mushroom pie. On Sundays, there is a three-course lunch with a choice of roasts and specials, all served with roast potatoes and fresh seasonal vegetables, plus a wide choice of desserts.

DICKENS CONNECTION

"The little pupils having been stimulated with the remains of their breakfast, and further invigorated by sundry small cups of a curious cordial carried by Mr. Squeers, which tasted very like toast-and-water put into a brandy bottle by mistake went to sleep, woke, shivered, and cried, as their feelings prompted. So the day wore on at Eton Slocomb there was a good coach dinner, of which the box, the four front outsides, the one inside, Nicholas, the good tempered man, Mr. Squeers partook, while the five little boys were put to thaw by the fire and regalled with sandwiches."

"Nicholas Nickleby"   Book I   Chpt. V.
Dickens changed the name Eaton Socon to Eton Slocomb.

The Dukes Head Hotel

13 Hall Quay
Great Yarmouth
Norfolk
NR30 1HP

Tel : 01493 859 184

HISTORY: The Dukes Head dates back to the 15th century.   Behind the knapped flint front are the remains of a half-timbered building.   A large oval moulded window jamb was found at first floor level and, behind the flints, the returns to the window revealed large disclosed bricks eleven inches in length, similar to the ones at Caister Castle.   One of the upper rooms is panelled in oak from floor to ceiling with a most elaborately carved chimney piece. The London-bound coach and four departed from the courtyard of this inn on Thursdays of every week at 11 o'clock; the fare was 50 shillings (£2.50), which was payable to the coach driver, and gentlemen were advised to carry their own personal bags to ensure that they did not go astray at the various stopping points on the journey.

BAR/RESTAURANT: The Dukes Head has a warm and cosy interior where you can enjoy staple pub food which is wholesome and freshly-cooked, such as steak and Guinness pie, scampi and chips or lasagne.   From the blackboard, choose your starter and desserts.   A good selection of sandwiches and baguettes is also available.

OPENING TIMES:

Monday - Saturday	10.00am -	3.00pm
	6.00pm -	9.00pm
Sunday	10.00am -	6.00pm

DIRECTIONS:
Town centre, near the quayside.

🚗 🍴 ⊗ ☺ 💳 VISA £ - ££

DICKENS CONNECTION

He brought me some chops, and vegetables, and took the covers off in such a bouncing manner that I was afraid I must have given him some offence. But he greatly relieved my mind by putting a chair for me at the table, and saying very affably, "Now, six-foot! come on!". I thanked him, and took my seat at the board; to handle my knife and fork with anything like dexterity, or to avoid splashing myself with the gravy, while he was standing opposite, staring so hard, and making me blush in the most dreadful manner every time I caught his eye. After watching me into the second chop, he said: "There's half a pint of ale for you. Will you have it now?" I thanked him and said "Yes." Upon which he poured it out of a jug into a large tumbler, and held it up against the light, and made it look beautiful. "My eye!" he said, "It seems a good deal, don't it?" "It does seem a good deal," I answered with a smile. For it was quite delightful to me to find him so pleasant. He was a twinkling-eyed, pimple-faced man, with his hair standing upright all over his head; and as he stood with one arm a-kimbo, holding up the glass to the light with the other hand, he looked quite friendly. "There was a gentleman here yesterday," he said - "a stout gentleman, by the name of Topsawyer - perhaps you know him?" "No," I said, "I don't think - " "In breeches and gaiters, broad-brimmed hat, grey coat, speckled choker," said the waiter. "No," I said bashfully, "I haven't the pleasure -" "He came in here," said the waiter, looking at the light through the tumbler, "ordered a glass of this ale - would order it - I told him not - drank it, and fell dead."

"David Copperfield"   Book I   Chpt. V

85

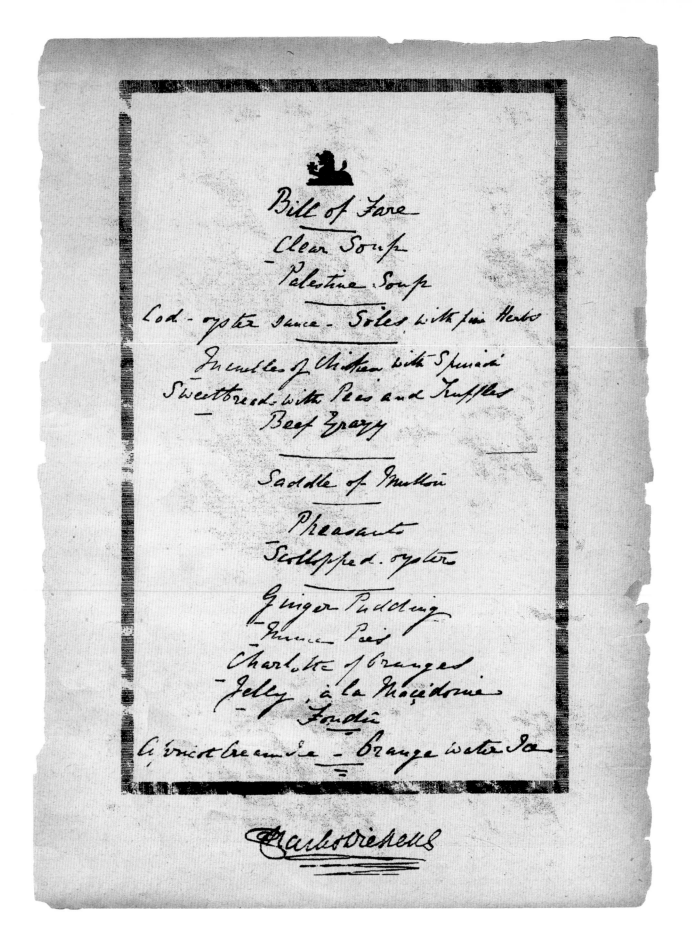

Bill of Fare
Clear Soup
Palestine Soup

Cod – oyster Sauce – Soles with fine Herbs

Rissoles of Chicken with Spinach
Sweetbread with Peas and Truffles
Beef Epargy

Saddle of Mutton

Pheasants
Scolloped oysters

Ginger Pudding
Mince Pies
Charlotte of Oranges
Jelly à la Macédoine
Fondu
Apricot Cream Ice – Orange water Ice

Charles Dickens

A copy of the menu written and signed by Charles Dickens
whilst staying at The Royal Hotel on one of his many visits.

The Royal Hotel

**Marine Parade
Great Yarmouth
Norfolk
NR30 4AE**

Tel : 01493 844 215
Fax : 01493 331 921

E-mail :
royalhotelgy@fsmail.net

HISTORY: The Royal Hotel, as it is now known, has been standing on the seafront for over 300 years. In the late 1700s, it was called the Victoria Hotel. The name was changed to Birds Royal Hotel & Posting House; the Palm Court being the pick-up-point for the Royal Mail and also for passengers for the London stagecoach. When the railways started to take the mail and passengers, "Posting House" was dropped from the name, hence the Royal Hotel. Many famous people have stayed at the hotel including Edward VII with Lily Langtry, and also Charles Dickens. He wrote to his wife saying that "Yarmouth was the most wondrous sight his eyes had ever beheld".

OLIVER'S TEA SHOP: Snacks are available all day, and delicious cream teas with all the trimmings.

BAR: Relax and enjoy hot snacks and a selection of sandwiches which are served in the bright and cheerful bar from 8pm until 11pm.

RESTAURANT: The spacious dining room offers a four-course table d'hôte dinner menu, which is changed daily and consists mainly of traditional food -- soups, pâté, fresh Lowestoft plaice, home-made pies, duck and chicken dishes, and a selection of roasts. All are served with seasonal vegetables, plus there's chef's choice of desserts and ice cream.

OPENING TIMES:

All week; mid March - mid October.

Breakfast	8.30am - 9.30am
Dinner	6.00pm - 7.00pm
Bar	8.00pm - 11.00pm

DIRECTIONS: The hotel is on the seafront at the southern end of Great Yarmouth.

ⓟ 🚭 ☺ ♯♯ ♿ 🚌 MasterCard VISA ⊡ £ - £££

DICKENS CONNECTION

*My Dearest Kate,
I received your letter here this morning, and was very glad (and a good deal relieved) to find that you were quite well when you wrote. We have had a two or three and twenty mile walk today- to Lowestoft in Suffolk (Mrs. Gibson's country) and back, and are sitting round the fire, giving encouragement to Lemon, who did his walking admirably, but is somewhat disposed to snore. He breaks into a snore in the most wonderful manner, instantly after he has been broad awake.*

Extract of a letter Charles Dickens wrote to his wife whilst staying at the Royal Hotel on 9th January 1849.

The Great White Horse Hotel

**Tavern Street
Ipswich
Suffolk
IP1 3AH**

Tel : 01473 256 558
Fax : 01473 253 396

E-mail : gwh@keme.co.uk

HISTORY: The Great White Horse is a grade II listed building dating back to the early 1500s in the reign of Henry VIII. There's no doubt that there was a resting house on the site for weary travellers long before that, which makes it the oldest and longest established business in Ipswich. During the peak of the coaching era in the 18th and 19th centuries, it was one of the most prestigious inns in East Anglia. The hotel has played host to many distinguished guests including Louis XVIII of France, Admiral Lord Nelson, and in January 1737, King George II, who rested overnight whilst on his way from Lowestoft to London. The King arrived at about 11.00pm and received the town dignitaries in one of the first floor reception rooms. The most illustrious person to be born in Ipswich was Cardinal Wolsey who was educated at the local grammar school and Magdalen College, Oxford. Charles Dickens stayed at the hotel whilst working for the *Morning Chronicle* as a reporter covering the Suffolk Parliamentary Elections.

BAR: In the attractive bar, there's a good selection of wholesome freshly-made snacks such as sandwiches and baguettes with various fillings.

RESTAURANT: The Courtyard Café with its glass covered roof is a popular place to eat in a comfortable and relaxed setting. Here, you can choose from an extensive menu with dishes such as garlic mushrooms with parsley mayonnaise, avocado, crab and crispy bacon salad; smoked salmon and scrambled eggs or pasta served with salmon and broccoli.

OPENING TIMES:

Bar/Restaurant:
All week   12.00am - 2.30pm
               6.30pm - 9.00pm

DIRECTIONS: Take A12 and follow signs to Ipswich town centre. Short distance from railway station.

Ⓟ ♦♦ ⊗ ☺ ♿ ▭▭ VISA ▭ £ - ££

DICKENS CONNECTION

"In the main street of Ipswich, on the left-hand side of the way, a short distance after you have passed through the open space fronting the town hall, stands an inn known far and wide by the appellation of The Great Horse, rendered the more conspicuous by a stone statue of some rampacious animal with flowing mane and tail, distantly resembling an insane cart-horse, which is elevated above the principal door."

"Pickwick Papers"   Book I   Chpt. XXII

The Village Maid

**71 The Street
Lound
Suffolk
NR32 5LP**

Tel : 01502 730 441

Web :
www.village-world.com

E-mail :
loundmaid@AOL.com.uk

HISTORY: The Village Maid was built in 1834 as a public house and stands in a pleasant setting opposite the village pond. The interior has been extended to a large open-plan area around the bar. Hanging on the walls are many interesting photographs of the pub.

OPENING TIMES:

Bar/Restaurant:

All week	11.30am - 2.00pm
	7.00pm - 9.00pm

DIRECTIONS:
Head for northern end of the village, opposite the pond. Approximately three miles miles from Oulton Broad.

BAR/RESTAURANT: In the comfortable, relaxed atmosphere you can enjoy a good selection of hot and cold food such as filled baguettes, sandwiches and jacket potatoes. Main courses include starters like hot and spicy prawns, breaded mushrooms and whitebait, followed by favourites such as mixed grills, hearty steaks, chops and a selection of fish. There's a good variety of mouth-watering desserts, which can be blueberry sponge, strawberry cheesecake, blackberry crumble, or death by chocolate. All the food is freshly-prepared to order.

DICKENS CONNECTION

"We made so many deviations up and down lanes, and were such a long time delivering a bedstead at a public-house, and calling at other places, that I was quite tired, and very glad, when we saw Yarmouth. It looked rather spongy and soppy, I thought, as I carried my eye over the great dull waste that lay across the river; and I could not help wondering, if the world were really as round as my geography-book said, how any part of it came to be so flat. But I reflected that Yarmouth might be situated at one of the poles; which would account for it."

"David Copperfield"   Book I   Chpt. III

The Eight Bells

**2 Park Street
Old Hatfield
Hertfordshire
AL9 5AX**

Tel : 01707 266 059

To Lovers of Charles Dickens

THIS EIGHT BELLS INN IS WITHOUT DOUBT
THAT SMALL PUBLIC HOUSE WHERE BILL SIKES
AND HIS DOG FOUND TEMPORARY REFUGE
AFTER THE BRUTAL MURDER OF NANCY.
IT WAS IN THE TAP ROOM THAT AN ANTIC
FELLOW, HALF PEDLAR AND HALF MOUNTEBANK
AFTER MENTIONING BLOODSTAINS, OFFERED
TO REMOVE THE STAINS FROM SIKES HAT.

OPENING TIMES:

Monday - Friday	12.00am -	3.00pm
	5.00pm -	8.00pm
Saturday - Sunday	12.00am -	4.00pm

DIRECTIONS:
Old Hatfield close to Hatfield House.

HISTORY: The Eight Bells (formerly The Five Bells) is situated in the picturesque village of Old Hatfield, just outside the grounds of Hatfield House. The House was built in 1497 for the Bishops of Ely. When Henry VIII dispersed the churches, he converted it and used the property as a residence for his children. Whilst working on the *Morning Chronicle*, Dickens was sent to Hatfield in 1835 to report on the great fire that began in the West wing. The first Marchioness of Salisbury, who married the Marquess in 1773, tragically lost her life in the fire. When he became a famous writer, Dickens was a regular house guest at both Hatfield and Knebworth.

BAR/RESTAURANT: With its partly-flagstoned floor and traditional decor, the interior is everything you would expect inside an English pub; the menu won't disappoint either; as well as the usual options, such as soup and jacket potatoes, there's a good selection of hot or cold chunky 'doorstep' sandwiches with delicious fillings -- everything from honey-roast ham to steak and onion, and tuna and cheese melt. The more substantial dishes on the menu can include favourites such as fish and chips or roasted Mediterranean lasagne, alongside spicier options like beef nachos, jalapeno dippers or Cajun chicken. For those who want a little more, try the all-day breakfast.

DICKENS CONNECTION

"He wandered over miles and miles of ground, and still came back to the old place. Morning and noon had passed, and the day was on the wane, and still he rambled to and fro, and up and down, and round and round, and still lingered about the same spot. At last he got away, and shaped his course for Hatfield. It was nine o'clock at night, when the man, quite tired out, and the dog, limping and lame from the unaccustomed exercise, turned down the hill by the church of the quiet village, and plodding along the little street, crept into a small public house, whose scanty light had guided them to the spot. There was a fire in the tap-room, and some country-labourers were drinking before it. They made room for the stranger, but he sat down in the farthest corner, and ate and drunk alone, or rather with his dog: to whom he cast a morsel of food from time to time."

"Oliver Twist" Chpt. XLVIII

The White Hart Hotel

**Holywell Hill
St. Albans
Hertfordshire
AL1 1EZ**

Tel : 01727 853 624

HISTORY: In the mid 9th century, the Roman Watling Street had been diverted from its route through Verulamium to pass around the Abbey; which, in effect, created Holywell Hill where the White Hart is situated. The oldest part of the inn dates back to 1500, but has been extended and adapted over the years. In 1535, it was known as the Hartshorn when it was leased by the Abbot of St. Albans to John Broke and his wife. In 1746, the Jacobite rebel Lord Lovat stayed at the inn on his way to the Tower of London after falling ill. He could not escape his fate, however, and was beheaded following his trial for treason. He was the last aristocrat to meet this end. In the 19th century, wall paintings were discovered in a house next to the inn which was originally part of the White Hart and were very large with designs including birds, animals and foliage and a painting showing the story of Venus and Adonis, based on a poem by William Shakespeare. In 1820, there was a tragic accident at the inn. On entering the carriageway, Elizabeth Wilson, seated on top of the Northampton coach, failed to duck as it swept under the entrance and was killed by the impact. The incident may well have provided the inspiration for Charles Dickens in *Pickwick Papers*, when Mr. Jingle tells the story to Samuel Pickwick.

BAR/RESTAURANT: This old inn has retained much of its old world atmosphere with its low ceiling and rich oak-panelled walls. The bar has a selection of light snacks, which include ciabatta rolls and crispy baguettes fillings include steak, onion and mushrooms or cheese and tomato. Potato wedges, combo platters consisting of chicken goujons, battered onion rings, crispy wedges, mushroom boats, chicken wings and garlic bread are also on offer. The attractive and spacious dining room serves main courses such as rump steak, gammon and eggs, various fish dishes and a selection of burgers. The Tower is two 4oz beef burgers topped with cheese, bacon, tomato, hash brown and fried egg. Desserts include chocolate fudge cake, apple pie and a choice from the chalk board. Roast dinners are also available on Sundays.

OPENING TIMES:

Bar/Restaurant:

All week	12.00am -	2.30pm
	6.00pm -	9.30pm

DIRECTIONS: In town centre by the Abbey.

DICKENS CONNECTION

"Heads, heads - take care of your heads!" cried the loquacious stranger, as they came out under the low archway, which in those days formed the entrance to the coach-yard. "Terrible place - dangerous work - other day- five children - mother - tall lady, eating sandwiches - forgot the arch - crash - knock - children look round - mother's head off - sandwiches in her hand - no mouth to put it in - head of a family off - shocking, shocking! Looking at Whitehall, Sir? - fine place - little window - somebody else's head off there, eh, sir? - he didn't keep a sharp look-out enough either - eh, sir. eh?" "I am ruminating," said Mr Pickwick, "on the strange mutability of human affairs." "Ah! I see - in at the palace door one day, out at the window the next. Philosopher, sir?" "An observer of human nature, sir," said Mr. Pickwick."

"Pickwick Papers"   Book I   Chpt. II
Dickens was a frequent visitor to St Albans.

The George

**71 St. Martins
Stamford
Lincolnshire
PE9 2LB**

Tel : 01780 750 750
Fax : 01780 750 701

Web : www.georgehotelofstamford.com
E-mail : reservations@georgehotelofstamford.com

HISTORY: The George is one of the great coaching inns of England, and is believed to be at least 1000 years old. In 1189, Richard Ist gave the Abbey of Peterborough a charter confirming their possession of the George Inn. The main block of the inn was rebuilt by Lord Burghley in 1597, and his coat of arms can still be seen over the front entrance. By the 17th and 18th centuries, the George had become a hostelry of great renown and was frequented by royalty and nobility. Charles Ist stayed in 1641 and 1645. The Duke of Cumberland stayed at the inn in 1745 after his victory at Culloden. During the 18th century, when the great turnpike roads were being built, no fewer than 40 coaches a day passed through Stamford. The "London Room" and the "York Bar" opposite were once waiting rooms for these coaches. Today, the George has retained the charm and atmosphere of its long history, whilst offering guests every modern comfort.

BAR/LOUNGE: The light and airy Garden Lounge has an informal atmosphere and serves a very wide choice of interesting and delicious food. To start, there's Gruyère cheese fritters with Thai jelly or Parma ham with a fennel salad, and a lime and olive dressing. For the main course, you could have a pasta dish from the very large selection or shellfish. If you have a good appetite, try the Grand Brittany Platter, which is half a lobster, crab, langoustine, king prawns, oysters, mussels, clams, shell-on prawns and whelks. Char-grilled steaks, chicken breasts and lambs' liver are also on the menu, plus a cold buffet which serves open Danish sandwiches, beef, ham, salmon and seafood salads. To finish, there's a choice of sweets, tarts, sorbets and ice cream.

RESTAURANT: The magnificent oak-panelled dining room offers an imaginative à la carte menu of mainly English dishes. Starters can include local game terrine with spiced pear chutney or pan-fried sea scallops on a pureé of smoked bacon and savoy cabbage with black pudding sauce. Main meals include a good choice of fish such as whole lobster, Dover sole and poached medley of seafood. There's a variety of game on the menu such as breast of guinea fowl, roast partridge or venison. Beef dishes include sirloin, and medallions of beef fillet. If you have room, there's a dessert and cheese trolley.

OPENING TIMES:
Bar/Restaurant:
   All week   12.00am - 10.30pm

DIRECTIONS:
Take the A1 to Stamford town centre.

DICKENS CONNECTION

The George was one of the great coaching inns on the Great North Road. On his many trips to the north of England, Charles Dickens would probably have stopped-over or rested at The George. One such trip was in February 1838 with his illustrator Hablot K. Browne. They were bound for Yorkshire to investigate the poor conditions in boarding schools which culminated in the publication of his novel Nicholas Nickleby.

The Bell Inn Hotel

7 High Street
Great North Road
Stilton
Peterborough
Cambridgeshire   PE7 3RA

Tel : 01733 241 066
Fax : 01733 245 173
Web : www.thebellstilton.co.uk
E-mail : reception@thebellstilton.co.uk

HISTORY: The Bell with its old world charm, exposed stone walls and beams, is said to be one of the finest surviving examples of a 17th century coaching inn. The present building dates from 1642, the date marked on the southern gable, and the year in which the Civil War began. Records show, however, that the inn has stood on the present site since 1437. During the heyday of the coaching era between the 1630s to 1840s, the inn was an important stop on the Great North Road between London and York. Coaches brought people and, of great importance, the mail. In the 1730s, an enterprising landlord sold cheese made by his sister-in-law who was housekeeper at nearby Quenby Hall. Soon the cheese's fame spread and the landlord named it Stilton after the village. Over the years, many famous people have stayed at the Bell including the Duke of Marlborough and Lord Byron, and during the Second World War, Clark Gable and Joe Louis visited whilst stationed at the nearby American Air Force base.

BAR: The Village Bar has a relaxing atmosphere with its stone floor and roaring log fire on chilly days. Here you are spoilt for choice with simple bar snacks to an excellent selection of starters and imaginative main courses. Try confit of duck with black pudding or grilled halibut on savoy cabbage with smoked salmon sauce. Puddings and cheeses are available from the "specials" board. In fine weather, meals can be eaten outside in the beautiful stone courtyard. There is also a cosy and comfortable residents' bar.

RESTAURANT: The beamed, galleried 16th century restaurant is delightful and offers superb modern British cuisine using the very best local produce for freshness and quality. Starters to tempt you can feature a warm salad of marinated artichokes or pigeon and pork faggots; mains include pan-fried calves' liver, warm tart of Stilton and spinach or roasted curried monkfish. Bread and butter pudding ice cream, or maybe prune and Armagnac tart are just a sample of the innovative puddings available.

OPENING TIMES:

Bar:

Monday - Saturday	12.00am -	2.00pm
	6.30pm -	9.30pm
Sunday	12.00am -	2.00pm
	7.00pm -	9.00pm

Restaurant:

Monday - Thursday	7.00pm -	9.30pm
Friday - Sunday	12.00am -	2.00pm

DIRECTIONS:
Leave the A1(M) at Norman Cross and take the B1043 to village centre.

£ - £££

DICKENS CONNECTION

"A stage or two further on, the lamps were lighted, and a great to-do occasioned by the taking up, at a road-side inn, of a very fastidious lady with an infinite variety of cloaks and small parcels, who loudly lamented, for the behoof of the outsides, the non-arrival of her own carriage which was to have taken her on."

"Nicholas Nickleby"   Book I   Chpt. V

White Horse

**North Street
Sudbury
Suffolk
CO10 1RF**

Tel : 01787 371 063

OPENING TIMES:

Monday (not evening)	11.30am -	3.00pm
Tuesday - Saturday	11.00am -	3.00pm
	5.00pm -	8.00pm
Sunday	12.00am -	3.00pm

DIRECTIONS:
A131/A14. Follow signs to town centre.

Ⓟ ⊗ ⊖ ♿ £ - ££

DICKENS CONNECTION

"Why doubtful, my dear sir; rather doubtful as yet," replied the little man. "Fizkin's people have got three-and-thirty voters in the lock-up coach-house at the White Hart." "In the coach-house!" said Mr. Pickwick, considerably astonished by this second stroke of policy. "They keep 'em locked up there till they want 'em," resumed the little man. "The effect of that is, you see, to prevent our getting at them; and even if we could, it would be of no use, for they keep them very drunk on purpose. Smart fellow Fizkin's agent - very smart fellow indeed. Mr. Pickwick stared, but said nothing. "We are pretty confident though," said Mr. Perker, sinking his voice almost to a whisper. "We had a little tea-party here, last night - five-and-forty women, my dear sir - and gave every one of 'em a green parasol when she went away." "A parasol!" said Mr. Pickwick."

"Pickwick Papers"   Book I   Chpt. XIII
Dickens called "The White Horse" the "White Hart"

HISTORY: This lovely old pub standing in the town centre dates back to the 16th century. It has old lock-up stables at the rear, which would suggest that it was previously a small coaching inn.

BAR: The bar has low ceilings and wood-panelled walls, and is a popular venue with the locals. There's an extensive choice of good wholesome food, ranging from generously-filled chunky sandwiches, toasted sandwiches, hot crispy French sticks, home-made soup, filled jacket potatoes served with mixed salad, to lighter meals such as salads or omelettes.   More substantial dishes can include pasta, burgers, fish and chips, grills and steaks. Desserts include home-made sherry trifle, fruit of the forest pavlova, pancakes and old favourites like apple pie.

Midlands & Wales

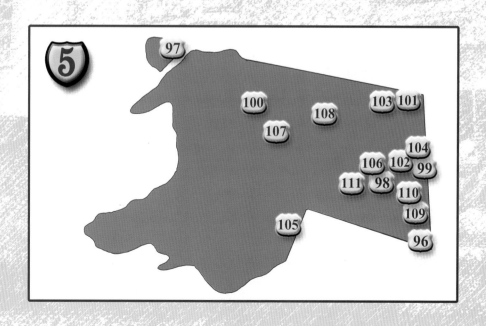

The King's Head

King's Head Passage
Market Square
Aylesbury
Buckinghamshire
HP20 2RW

Tel : 01296 718 812

HISTORY: The King's Head is a wonderful, historically significant building. It is part of a rich English history from the Civil War dating back to Henry VI and the War of the Roses. The earliest documented date for the inn is 1455, when it probably served as a guesthouse for visitors to the nearby Greyfriars Monastery. The inn has always been known as The King's Head; the king in question being Henry VI whose coat of arms and those of his wife are still preserved with other 15th century glass in the Great Hall. In 1650, it was the premier coaching inn and became the first posting house in Aylesbury. During the Civil War, Aylesbury was a Parliamentary stronghold and Oliver Cromwell is thought to have used the inn as his headquarters for the battle of Aylesbury in 1642. A number of items reputedly related to him include a chair in a room that bears his name, and these can still be seen today. The last owner was The Hon. Charles Rothschild's widow, and the family passed it to The National Trust in 1925. In October 2000, it was once again let as a public house.

BAR/RESTAURANT: The attractive room with its Georgian panelling and pretty stained glass windows provides a relaxing setting in which to enjoy a good selection of food. Starters can be soup of the day, tomato and mozzarella salad or pâté and toast. Mains include delicious home-made sausages with sage, mashed potato and onion gravy, grilled lambs' liver and bacon, plus chicken dishes, steak or omelettes. There's also the all-day breakfast.

OPENING TIMES:

Bar/Restaurant

Monday - Saturday	11.30am -	2.30pm
Sunday	12.00am -	2.30pm

<u>No food served in the evening.</u>

DIRECTIONS:
Town centre -- off the Market Square.

£ - ££

DICKENS CONNECTION

"In this way they travelled on until near midnight, when they stopped to supper, for which meal the single gentleman ordered everything eatable that the house contained; and because Kit's mother didn't eat everything at once, and eat it all, he took it into his head that she must be ill. "I see what's the matter with you, ma'am. You're faint." "You're faint," said the single gentleman, who did nothing himself but walk about the room. "Thank you, sir, I'm not indeed." "I know you are, I'm sure of it, I drag this poor woman from the bosom of her family at a minute's notice, and she goes on getting fainter and fainter before my eyes."

"The Old Curiosity Shop"   Book II   Chpt. XLVII

Ye Olde Bull's Head Inn

Castle Street
Beaumaris
Anglesey
Gwynedd
LL58 8AP

Tel : 01248 810 329
Fax : 01248 811 294

Web : www.bullsheadinn.co.uk

E-mail : info@bullsheadinn.co.uk

HISTORY: The inn was established in 1472 and rebuilt in 1617, and was the original posting house of the borough and a staging post on the route to Ireland. The inn was commandeered by General Mytton who besieged Beaumaris Castle during the Parliamentary invasion of Royalist Wales in 1645-1646. Famous guests who have stayed at the inn include Dr. Samuel Johnson and Charles Dickens who was a guest here while reporting the sinking of the Royal Charter off the Anglesey coast, which happened on 26th October 1859.

RESTAURANT/BRASSERIE: The elegant upstairs dining room offers creative modern British cuisine using fine local produce which can include starters like venison salad with raisins, hazelnuts and balsamic vinegar; twice-baked Gorau glas cheese soufflé with a chive cream and artichokes. Mains can be loin of Welsh lamb with borlotti beans, lamb confit and smoked garlic, and roast breast of Hereford duck with sweet potato flan, baby turnips and red port. For a more informal menu, head for the hotel's brasserie. Competitively-priced dishes include starters such as char-grilled ostrich burger and smoked haddock chowder, plus a comprehensive selection of mains to follow. Take your pick from pasta dishes, sandwiches and some unusual salads, such as chicken liver and bacon with mixed leaves and balsamic vinegar. There's also a good choice of game and meat dishes, as well as locally-caught seafood. Try the steamed mussels with smoked bacon or creamy cassolette of seafood with dill, fennel and puff pastry. If you've got room, the puddings and cheeses won't disappoint, such as sloe gin jelly with

home-made shortbread. A large selection of wine from around the world is available.

OPENING TIMES:

Restaurant:
  All week   7.00pm - 9.30pm

Brasserie:
  All week   12.00am - 2.00pm
                                6.00pm - 9.00pm

DIRECTIONS:
From Britannia Road Bridge (A5) follow the A545 for approximately five miles.

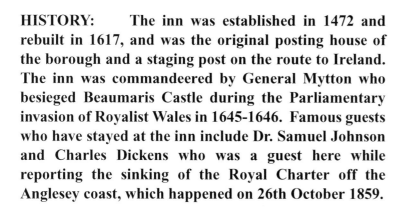

DICKENS CONNECTION

Charles Dickens stayed at the Ye Olde Bull's Head whilst reporting on the catastrophic sinking of the Royal Charter. The ship left Melbourne on the 26th August, making a record homeward journey. The Captain was asked to make a diversion to Holyhead as some of the passengers wished to see the Great Eastern, which was the largest ship in the world at this time. He agreed to this request but, unfortunately, at about 7.00am on the 26th October 1859 the ship was caught in a violent storm and she broke in two. 459 passengers and crew were drowned, including the captain. Dickens wrote a story based on this event called "The Shipwreck".

"The Uncommercial Traveller" Chpt. II

The Dun Cow

The Green
Dunchurch
Rugby
Warwickshire
CV22 6NJ

Tel : 01788 810 305
Fax : 01788 810 931

HISTORY: Dating from the 17th century, the Dun Cow stands on the old Roman road -- Watling Street. It was a major staging post where horses were changed en route to make the long journey to Holyhead. The Dun Cow's reputation for traditional hospitality has attracted many famous guests over the years. It is known that railway engineer Robert Stephenson and his father, George, met at the Dun Cow in 1837 to celebrate the completion of the nearby Kilsby Tunnel. Local legend has it that Henry Wadsworth Longfellow wrote *The Village Blacksmith* whilst staying here in 1840. Nearby is a house that was originally a pub called The Red Lion where the conspirators of the gunpowder plot met.

BAR/RESTAURANT: With its warm and welcoming atmosphere, you can enjoy a selection of ingredients from around the world cooked in a distinctly British style. There is a wide variety of basics: sandwiches, soup, breaded mushrooms and salads. Main courses can be sausages and Cheddar mash, chicken dishes, rump or gammon steaks, pies, scampi and chips, which are all served with fresh seasonal vegetables. Delicious roasts are available on Sundays. There is a good choice of puddings served from the trolley. In fine weather, meals can be eaten in the attractive beer garden.

OPENING TIMES:

Bar/Restaurant:
Monday - Saturday   12.00am - 10.00pm

Sunday   12.00am - 9.30pm

DIRECTIONS: From the A45 take the A426 to Dunchurch. The Dun Cow is on the main road in the town centre.

£ - £££

DICKENS CONNECTION

"This here," replied Sam, without goin' so far as to as-sert, as some wery sensible people do, that postboys and donkeys is both immortal, Wot I say is this; That wenever they feels theirselves gettin' stiff and past their work, they just rides off together, wun postboy to a pair in the usual way; wot becomes on 'em nobody knows, but it's weary probable as they starts away to take their pleasure in some other world, for there ain't a man alive as ever see, either a donkey or a postboy, a takin' his pleasure in this!" Expatiating upon this learned and remarkable theory, and citing many curious statistical and other facts in its support, Sam Weller beguiled the time until they reached Dunchurch, where a dry postboy and fresh horses were procured; the next stage was Daventry and the next Towcester; and at the end of each stage it rained harder than it had done at the beginning."

"Pickwick Papers"   Book II   Chpt. LI

The Star Inn

2 Bridge Street
Geddington
Northamptonshire
NN14 1AD

Tel : 01536 742 386

HISTORY: The Star is a 14th century inn standing in the village square. Opposite the inn stands Eleanor Cross which was built by Edward Ist in memory of his beloved Queen Eleanor. The Queen had died in 1290 at Harby in Nottinghamshire and the King brought her body to London to be buried in Westminster Abbey. The mourning King erected a cross at each of the places where the coffin rested overnight -- 12 in all. Geddington is by far the best preserved of the only three still remaining. The famous water splash that Dickens mentioned is about 100 yards away from the inn; it can be seen from the bridge over the river Ise.

BAR/RESTAURANT: In the small, comfortable bar there is a wide variety of good wholesome food including sandwiches, rolls and salads. Main meals are served in the dining area and feature a choice of starters with main courses such as mixed grill, steaks or a seafood platter. A choice of desserts is available from the chalk boards. The restaurant also offers a good selection of authentic Greek dishes.

OPENING TIMES:

Bar:		
Tuesday - Sunday	12.00am -	3.00pm
	6.00pm -	9.00pm
Restaurant:		
Tuesday - Sunday	12.00am -	2.00pm
	6.00pm -	9.00pm

Closed on Mondays.

DIRECTIONS: Turn off A43 to Geddington.

£ - ££

DICKENS CONNECTION

"We started at about 11 o'clock for the Duke of Buccleugh's seat which is about 4 or 5 miles from hence, dined at a country public-house, and returned after dark, when our driver being very near-sighted and slightly over-come with potations of ale, and egg flip, ingeniously drove the party into a "water splash". The guard dismounted - the water being up to the calves of his legs - and after a great deal of dragging, splashing, and shouting, succeeded in leading the horse back to the road, and we all arrived here in time for coffee. On the preceding day I was at Northampton. And now my dear girl I have only time to add that business and want of space combined, compel me to close my letter abruptly."

"Extract from a letter Charles Dickens sent to Catherine Hogarth dated 18th December 1835 from the White Hart - Kettering (now gone).

The Hand Hotel

Bridge Street
Llangollen
Clwyd
LL20 8PL

Tel : 01978 860 303
Fax : 01978 861 277

Web :
www.peelhotel.com

E-mail :
info@hand-hotel-llangollen.com

HISTORY: Built in 1700, the Hand Hotel was an important post house in the days of the Irish mail coaches that travelled to and from London to the Irish ports. Several public houses and hotels in the locality are called The Hand or Red Hand, one theory as to why this is so relates to a story of two men from important families fighting for power and deciding the outcome on a race to the English border. One of the men became weak and exhausted but, wanting to win the race badly, chopped off his hand with his sword and thrust it across the border, thus becoming the champion. Many notable people have stayed at the hotel including The Duke of Wellington, William Wordsworth, Robert Browning, Sir Walter Scott, Lord Tenyson and Charles Dickens. Nowadays, guests are lucky enough to be entertained several times a week by the splendid Llangollen Male Voice Choir, who practise at the hotel and often have a singalong in the bar after rehearsals.

BAR: The warm and inviting bar is a popular venue for locals and visitors alike, and offers a selection of snacks, such as sandwiches and baguettes filled with ham, tuna or Greenland prawns. For something hot, try chicken and bacon melt or sauté mushrooms glazed with Cheddar cheese. A carvery is served on Sundays with all the trimmings.

RESTAURANT: The attractive dining room overlooking the gardens and the River Dee has a set menu of mainly British food, with starters such as home-made mushroom soup finished with tarragon cream, or chicken liver pâté with cider and onion chutney. Main courses may be honey-roast gammon and parsley sauce, and oven-baked salmon fillet topped by capers and prawns in lemon butter. Desserts include old favourites like bread and butter pudding, sherry trifle or strawberry gâteau and cream.

OPENING TIMES:

Bar:
   All week   12.00am - 4.00pm

Restaurant:
   All week   6.30pm - 8.30pm

DIRECTIONS: Turn off A5 to town centre.

DICKENS CONNECTION

Charles Dickens stayed at the hotel on 2nd November 1838. He was touring Wales with his illustrator Hablot K. Browne. His bill amounted to £1. 10s 0d.

The Reindeer Inn

22 Main Street
Long Bennington
Newark
Nottinghamshire
NG23 5EH

Tel : 01400 281 382

Web :
www.reindeerinn.co.uk

E-mail :
enquires@reindeerinn.co.uk

HISTORY: This attractive 17th century coaching inn is on the main street in the pretty village of Long Bennington just off The Great North Road. It was a popular stopping place to rest the horses and revive weary, hungry travellers.

BAR: In the cosy bar, there's a wide choice of delicious savoury sandwiches or baguettes with fillings such as chicken and mild curry mayonnaise, smoked salmon, cream cheese, paprika and lemon, and Stilton and celery; plus side orders of chips, spicy curly fries and garlic bread.

RESTAURANT: The dining room of this award-winning inn is attractively decorated, and provides a relaxing setting for guests to choose from a very extensive menu of English and International cuisine. To begin, try deep-fried whitebait dusted with paprika, smoked chicken and pine nut salad with an orange vinaigrette, or fresh melon with fruit coulis and berries. Main meals include Bristol bird -- a tender breast of chicken cooked in sherry, cream and mushrooms or fillet belvoir -- consisting of strips of fillet steak pan-fried with garlic, onions, Stilton, mushrooms and cream. A good choice of fish is available from the daily "special" board. To finish, there's a wide choice of naughty-but-nice puddings, such as maple and pecan pie, dark chocolate truffle torte, or locally-made farmhouse ice cream.

OPENING TIMES:

Bar/Restaurant:
  Monday - Saturday   12.00am - 3.00pm
                        7.00pm - 11.00pm

<u>Sunday -- no food available.</u>

DIRECTIONS:
Just off the A1 Great North Road between Grantham and Newark.

DICKENS CONNECTION

"They found on reaching it that it was a lonely place with no great accommodation in the way of apartments - that portion of its resources being all comprised in one public room with a sanded floor, and a chair or two, However, a large faggot and a plentiful supply of coals being heaped upon the fire, the appearance of things was not long in mending; and, by the time they had washed off all effaceable marks of the late accident, the room was warm and light, which was a most agreeable exchange for the cold and darkness out of doors."

"Nicholas Nickleby"   Book I   Chpt. VI

The Three Swans Hotel

High Street
Market Harborough
Leicestershire
LE16 7NJ

Tel : 01858 466 644
Fax : 01858 433 101

Web : www.threeswans.co.uk
E-mail : sales@threeswans.co.uk

HISTORY: For more than 500 years, this 16th century coaching inn has extended a warm welcome to travellers. It has also been visited by many royals, including King Charles Ist, the day before the Battle of Naseby in 1645 in The English Civil War, and Queen Anne, Princess of Denmark, in 1688. The earliest reference to the swans was in the will of Richard Cade, dated 27th November 1517, when it was a hostelry known as "Ye Sygne of Swanne". The second and third swans were added at a later date. The sign overhanging the High Street was made in the 17th century and is a fine example of the blacksmith's craft.

BAR/LOUNGE: The large and comfortable Fothergill Bar and Lounge has a portrait of a former owner of the hotel who was a well-known eccentric named John Fothergill. Traditional ales and a selection of crisps and snacks are served in this bar.

RESTAURANT: There are two dining rooms. The conservatory has a less formal setting where lunch is served, and during the summer months you can eat alfresco in the beautiful courtyard. The comfortable and elegant Swans Restaurant is recognised throughout the area for excellent food, wine and service, and offers extensive table d'hôte and à la carte menus. Starters can be savoury tartlet filled with collops of lobster; asparagus and egg presented with a lime-scented salad, or curls of Parma ham presented on a bed of crisp chicory garnished with blue cheese and walnuts. Main courses include ballantine of duck with thyme and onion stuffing served on roasted new potatoes with a Grand Marnier sauce, or fillet of sole with crab and spring onions poached in white wine with fennel sauce. To finish, there's a choice of desserts of the day or the cheese board.

OPENING TIMES:
All week

Bar:	11.00am -	11.00pm
Conservatory:	11.30am -	2.15pm
Restaurant:	12.00am -	2.30pm
	7.00pm -	9.30pm

DIRECTIONS:
A508 to Market Harborough town centre.

£ - £££

DICKENS CONNECTION

"Late in the afternoon we came to the market-town where we were to alight from the coach - a dull little town, with a church-spire, and a market-place, and a market-cross, and one intensely sunny street, and a pond with an old horse cooling his legs in it, and a very few men sleepily lying and standing about in narrow little bits of shade. After the rustling of the leaves and the waving corn all along the road, it looked as still, as hot, as motionless a little town as England could produce. At the inn, we found Mr. Boythorn on horseback, waiting with an open carriage, to take us to his house, which was a few miles off."

"Bleak House" Book I Chpt. XVIII

Comfort Hotel (Formerly The George)

George Street
Nottingham
Nottinghamshire
NG1 3BP

Tel : 0115 9475 641
Fax : 0115 9483 292

E-mail :
admin@gb620.u-net.com

HISTORY: This traditional town house was built in 1822 in the reign of George IV for the Duke of Rutland, and was later sold by him to become a hotel called "The George". It has recently been fully refurbished and renamed Comfort Hotel. It is situated in the city centre near the lively and thriving lace market. In 1912, Henry Fielding Dickens K.C., Charles Dickens' son, gave a reading of *A Christmas Carol* at the hotel to the Nottingham Mechanics Institute to commemorate the centenary of his father's birth on February 2nd 1812.

BAR: In the comfortable and pleasant bar, you can choose from snacks such as sandwiches and baguettes, which are available all day. Alternatively, pop in for just a refreshing cup of tea or coffee.

RESTAURANT: The elegant Duke's Restaurant offers a choice of cuisine from the à la carte and table d'hôte menus plus local specialities. Main dishes can range from sirloin and fillet steaks served with Diane or peppercorn sauce to chicken supreme or poached salmon with hollandaise sauce. The highlight of the menu is beef Wellington; fillet beef wrapped in pâté and puff pastry and served with Madeira sauce. There's a good variety of starters and desserts, plus a cheese board selection.

OPENING TIMES:

Bar:

All week	All day

Restaurant:

All week	7.00pm - 9.45pm

DIRECTIONS:

M1 J25. Follow signs to Nottingham city centre, take left fork at Talbot Street and go past Hilton Hotel. Get in left-hand lane and just past Boots the chemist, turn right into George Street.

£ - £££

DICKENS CONNECTION

Charles Dickens stayed at The George (recently renamed Comfort Hotel) whilst on a reading tour of the Midlands.

Sondes Arms

**Main Street
Rockingham
Market Harborough
Northamptonshire
LE16 9TG**

Tel : 01536 770 312
Fax : 01536 770 312

HISTORY: This charming old coaching inn with its mellow stone exterior has stood in the pleasant village of Rockingham for several hundred years. In 1849, Charles Dickens stayed at nearby Rockingham Castle with the Hon. Richard Watson and his wife. Both men shared similar liberal temperaments and became life-long friends. Dickens dedicated his novel *David Copperfield* to the Watsons. Also, in *Bleak House*, the Watsons became Lord and Lady Dedlock, whilst Rockingham Castle and the village were called Chesney Wold; and the Sondes Arms became the Dedlock Arms.

BAR: The lovely old bar with its beamed ceilings and open fire has a very large choice of delicious, freshly-prepared food. This ranges from sandwiches and baguettes served with salad and corn chips to jacket potatoes. There's also a wide variety of main courses, grills and house "specials" which can be salmon and tiger prawn wrap, breasts of pheasant plus chicken or lobster. Desserts can be selected from the blackboard.

RESTAURANT: The dining room has a warm and inviting atmosphere and offers an extensive à la carte menu with many imaginative starters such as steamed asparagus spears with a béarnaise sauce or avocado and tiger prawns served on a crisp salad. Main courses can include boned, rolled honey-roasted rack of lamb with a minted jus, tuna steak flamed in brandy or smoked chicken stroganoff. There is also a selection of grilled steaks with home-made sauces plus a choice of mouth-watering desserts such as chocolate truffle and orange cheesecake, strawberry charlotte or profiteroles.

OPENING TIMES:
Bar:

All week	12.00am - 2.30pm

Restaurant:

All Week	6.30pm - 9.30pm

DIRECTIONS: On the A6003 near Corby.

£ - £££

DICKENS CONNECTION

"Oh! if you please, miss," said Charley in a whisper, with her eyes at their roundest and largest. "You're wanted at the Dedlock Arms." "Why, Charley," said I, "who can possibly want me at the public house?" "I don't know, miss," returned Charley, putting her head forward, and folding her hands tight upon the band of her little apron; which she always did, in the enjoyment of anything mysterious or confidential, "but it's a gentleman, miss, and his compliments, and will you please to come without saying anything about it." "Whose compliments, Charley?" "His'n, miss", returned Charley: whose grammatical education was advancing, but not very rapidly. "And how do you come to be the messenger, Charley?" "I am not the messenger, if you please, miss," returned my little maid. "It was W. Grubble, miss." "And who is W. Grubble, Charley?" "Mister Grubble, miss," returned Charley. "Don't you know, miss? The Dedlock Arms, by W. Grubble," which Charley delivered as if she were slowly spelling out the sign. "Aye? the landlord, Charley?"

"Bleak House"   Book II   Chpt. XXXVII
Dickens called the "Sondes Arms" the "Dedlock Arms"

104

The Royal Hotel

Palace Pound
Ross-on-Wye
Herefordshire
HR9 5HZ

Tel : 01989 565 105
Fax : 01989 768 058

E-mail :
royal.rossonwye@oldenglishinns.co.uk

HISTORY: The Royal Hotel was built in 1837 and was one of the first hotels to cater for the new tourist trend; to this day it retains much of the Victorian grandeur associated with that era. Standing high on a sandstone bluff with spectacular views of the surrounding valley and horseshoe bend of the River Wye and the Welsh mountains beyond, the hotel is just a short walk from the centre of this delightful market town. The Royal has been associated with many famous people, including Charles Dickens, King George IV and Lloyd George. Queen Victoria stayed for afternoon tea and, more recently, entertainers Anne Robinson, Jeremy Beadle and June Whitfield. The hotel was used for the television series Miss Marple.

BAR/LOUNGE: In the comfortable lounge and bar, a wide range of light bites and hot meals are served such as freshly-baked baguettes with a choice of fillings, pâté, soup, and potato skins. Main meals can be poached salmon, gammon steak, pork and leek sausages, plus a selection of mouth-watering puddings. Afternoon cream tea is also available.

RESTAURANT: In the elegant Shires Restaurant, you can enjoy excellent cuisine chosen from either the à la carte or table d'hôte menus, such as beef Wellington, honey and apple glazed pork collops, or Barbary duck breast; all served with potatoes and vegetables of the day. There is an imaginative range of delicious starters and puddings including individual white chocolate and raspberry mousse laced with mango coulis, and deep-dish apple flan with sugared nuts and creamy custard sauce.

OPENING TIMES:

Bar/Restaurant:
All week	12.00am -	2.00pm
	7.00pm -	9.30pm

DIRECTIONS:
M50 to J4 and head for Ross-on-Wye.

£ - £££

DICKENS CONNECTION

Charles Dickens stayed at the hotel in September 1867 where he met his good friend and biographer John Forster, to discuss and arrange his second tour to America.

Three Horse Shoes Hotel

Sheep Street
Rugby
Warwickshire
CV21 3BX

Tel : 01788 544 585
Fax : 01788 546 097

HISTORY: Situated in the heart of historic Rugby town centre, this large and imposing coaching inn dates back 350 years. Rugby School is close by, which has many famous literary connections as well as being the birth place of Rugby football.

BAR/LOUNGE: The large comfortable bar and lounge with its cosy log fire offers a selection of hot and cold food.   Choose from sandwiches and baguettes with tasty fillings such as coronation chicken and tuna mayonnaise through to traditional ploughman's lunches and a variety of salads. Main meals include staples like jacket potatoes and omelettes, as well as more filling menu options. These range from green Thai lamb curry and peppered sirloin steak to pizza and fish dishes. There's also a further selection of chef's "specials" of the day from the blackboard.

RESTAURANT: The warm and inviting dining room has a fine Inglenook fireplace and many oak beams; the low-lights give it an intimate atmosphere. The menu offers a good range of English and International dishes, including roasted joints served with all the trimmings. There's also a four-course table d'hôte menu, which is changed every week and may include Lancashire hot pot, poached fillet of haddock, braised beef in beer and a choice of starters and desserts. All the food is freshly-prepared from local produce. Don't forget the great value week-day lunch menu -- three courses for under a tenner.

OPENING TIMES:
Bar/Restaurant:

Monday - Saturday	12.00am -	2.00pm
	6.00pm -	9.00pm
Sunday	12.00am -	5.00pm

DIRECTIONS: Take A428 to town centre.

🚗 ♟ ⊗ ♿ 💳 💳 £ - ££

DICKENS CONNECTION

"So, he announced at the Inn that he was "going to stay on for the present," and improved his acquaintance with the Junction that night, and again next morning, and again next night and morning: going down to the station, mingling with the people there, looking about him down all the avenues of railway, and beginning to take an interest in the incomings and outgoings of the trains. At first, he often put his head into Lamp's little room, but he never found Lamps there.   A pair or two of velveteen shoulders he usually found there, stooping over the fire, sometimes in connection with a clasped knife and a piece of bread and meat; but the answer to his inquiry "where's Lamps?" was, either that he was "t'other side the line," or, that it was his off-time, or (in the latter case) his own personal introduction to another Lamps who was not his lamps."

"Christmas Stories" Book II Mugby Junction Chpt I
Charles Dickens called Rugby "Mugby".

The Lion Hotel

Wyle Cop
Shrewsbury
Shropshire
SY1 1UY

Tel : 01743 353 107
Fax : 01743 352 744

Web : www.corushotels.com

E-mail : thelion@corushotels.com

HISTORY: The Lion Hotel, situated in the heart of Shrewsbury, was once a renowned coaching inn dating back to 1618, although parts of the building date back to the 14th and 15th centuries. During the 18th century, a grand ballroom was constructed which was designed in the style of Robert Adam. It was the social centre of the area, as London and Bath were too far away for the local nobility and gentry. Prince William of Gloucester stayed at the hotel in 1803 and attended a grand ball given in his honour. Many famous people have also enjoyed the hospitality of the hotel and these include Benjamin Disraeli, Madam Tussaud and singer Jenny Lind. Paganini gave two concerts in the Assembly Room. Charles Dickens also stayed at The Lion on several occasions.

BAR/LOUNGE: The bar and lounge are comfortably furnished with blazing log fires in the colder months. You'll find a wide choice of hot and cold food including roast beef, ham, Brie and salami, or turkey and cranberry sandwiches garnished with coleslaw; other dishes to try include salad, soup, chicken liver pâté and jacket potatoes. Main meals can be anything from battered deep-fried cod with chips and mushy peas to Thai green chicken curry or rump steak, and a selection of side dishes.

RESTAURANT: The Shires Restaurant offers a table d'hôte menu for both lunch and dinner. To start, there's a good choice such as crab and smoked mackerel mousse served with a lemon mayonnaise or fanned honeydew melon, accompanied by segments of blush grapefruit, drizzled with an orange and Malibu sauce. Mains can be roast of the day through to more exotic tastes, such as tempura vegetables and pork stroganoff cooked with paprika and flamed in brandy. To finish, treat yourself to one of the chef's home-made desserts.

OPENING TIMES:

Bar/Restaurant:
All week   12.30pm - 2.00pm
                     7.00pm - 9.00pm

DIRECTIONS: Head for town centre.

🚗 ⊖ ⊗ ♕ 💳 VISA 🔲 £ - £££

DICKENS CONNECTION

Charles Dickens stayed at the hotel on 1st November 1838 whilst touring the Midlands and North Wales with his illustrator H.K. Browne.

The Swan Hotel

46/46a Greengate Street
Stafford
Staffordshire
ST16 2JA

Tel : 01785 258 142
Fax : 01785 223 372

Web : www.theswanstafford.co.uk
E-mail : info@theswanstafford.co.uk

HISTORY: The present outline of The Swan Hotel hides the fact that it was originally two separate buildings which historians believe were on the site of old monastic college premises. Records show that in 1711 there were two houses, and one was called The Swan. By 1752, these two houses had been combined, probably by the construction of the archway that was the entrance to a large yard at the rear, and with the provision of rooms above, they became The Swan Hotel. King Charles Ist stayed at the hotel. His room, with its fine Jacobean oak panelling, can still be seen today. There's also an extensive system of cellars and a priest hole was discovered in an upstairs room adjacent to that in which King Charles had slept. There's a room in the basement that has not yet been explored, but is believed it could give access to a secret passage into the yard or outbuildings. With the arrival of the railways, this old coaching inn declined, as did the town. Charles Dickens stayed at the hotel in 1852 and called it "The Dodo". The hotel has recently undergone major renovation, and offers modern facilities whilst retaining many of its original features.

BAR/COFFEE SHOP: Laze away a morning in the coffee shop or bar and enjoy some light bites with your tea or cappuccino. Choose from a sausage, bacon and cheese pannini to the "early bird" continental breakfast or bowl of fresh fruit salad. Other options on the menu include tasty, innovative sandwiches, such as chicken and tuna melt with anchovy and coriander mayonnaise. On warmer days, eat al fresco in the pretty courtyard.

RESTAURANT: The award-winning brasserie offers contemporary English cooking and includes a children's menu, blow-out breakfasts, a fixed-price selection as well as a comprehensive choice of mouth-watering dishes. Start with steamed mussels cooked in shallots and lemon or a warm aubergine and goat's cheese tian with Parmesan crackling. Simple, but delicious mains include lamb shank with minted mash, grilled seabass in a sorrel and Pernod sauce, and medallions of beef with herb polenta. You'll also find pasta dishes, salads and side orders to tempt you, along with some perfect puds to end the meal. Highlights include bread and butter pudding and chocolate brúlée. Don't forget to savour the impressive wine list.

OPENING TIMES:
Bar/Coffee shop:
    All week   8.00am - 6.00pm
Brasserie:
    Monday - Saturday 12.00am - 10.00pm
    Sunday   12.00am - 9.00pm

DIRECTIONS: M6 J13 to town centre.

DICKENS CONNECTION

"Over the way, opposite to the staring blank bow windows of the Dodo, are a little ironmonger's shop, a little tailor's shop (with a picture of the fashions in the small window and a bandy-legged baby on the pavement staring at it)."

"Reprinted Pieces" - A Plated Article
Dickens called "The Swan" "The Dodo"

The Cock Hotel

72 High Street
Stony Stratford
Buckinghamshire
MK11 1AH

Tel : 01908 567 733
Fax : 01908 562 109

HISTORY: The Cock has stood on the old Roman road Watling Street (now the High Street) since 1470. During the English Civil War, the inn was used for quartering the troops, and because of the strategic importance of the town, it was fought over by both sides. 1742 saw the great fire of Stony Stratford, which was started by a chambermaid in the adjacent Bull Inn. Fearful that she would lose her position for burning a sheet while ironing, she stuffed it up the chimney, starting a blaze that rapidly spread and engulfed the east side of the street destroying both inns and the old church of Mary Magdalene. When the Cock was rebuilt, it incorporated a magnificent portico that came from nearby Stowe Palace, and a wealth of wrought ironwork projecting over the street, all of which can still be seen today. During the heyday of coach travel in the 18/19th centuries, there were as many as one hundred coaches coming into the town each day. The inn was the official staging post for the Manchester Flier, with a twenty-five minute stop for dinner. Travellers stopping at the Cock and also the Bull vied with each other telling outrageous stories of their travels, giving rise to the well-known phrase "a cock and bull story". The Cock features in nursery rhymes too. Travellers could hire horses from the inns and it was a "cock horse" that one hired to ride to Banbury Cross.

BAR: The large and comfortable Market Bar features a gallery of old photographs and other memorabilia detailing the town's past history. A wide range of dishes feature, including smoked salmon and cream cheese with red onions on a toasted ciabatta roll, bacon and mushroom melt, a choice of salads, and traditional dishes like speciality sausages with mashed potato and onion gravy, or fresh haddock in a light beer batter with chips. In fine weather, you can eat in the attractive courtyard.

RESTAURANT: The intimate brasserie boasts an innovative à la carte menu with starters such as chicken liver and wild mushroom parfait with Riesling jelly and toasted bocata or duo of salmon set in a tian with avocado and caper salsa. Main courses can be pan-fried beef fillet mignons with shiitake mushrooms, parsnip and potato purée and port wine jus, grilled fillets of seabass presented on asparagus spears with a coriander and lime dressing, and tempting desserts like dark chocolate truffle torte, and mixed berry pancakes with crème anglaise.

OPENING TIMES:

Bar/Restaurant:

Monday - Saturday	12.00am -	2.00pm
	6.30pm -	10.00pm
Sunday	12.00am -	3.00pm
	6.30pm -	9.30pm

DIRECTIONS:
J15 off M1. Take A508 to town centre.

£ - £££

DICKENS CONNECTION

Charles Dickens stayed on several occasions. Mr. Turveydrop, a character in Dickens' novel Bleak House is based on Stony Stratford resident Joseph Hambling who ran a dancing school in the town.

The Saracen's Head Hotel

219 Watling Street
Towcester
Northamptonshire
NN12 7BX

Tel : 01327 350 414
Fax : 01327 359 879

HISTORY: The Saracen's Head was built more than 400 years ago to provide food and also accommodation for any weary travellers. The hotel stands in the town centre on the great military road that ran from London to Holyhead, which the Romans called Watling Street. In the first century AD, the Romans developed a walled town called Lacotodorum alongside this road and this is now modern-day Towcester.

BAR/LOUNGE: The split-level bar offers three distinct areas of relaxation where a very large choice of delicious hot and cold snacks and main meals are available. Choose from sandwiches, baguettes, filled jacket potatoes, pizza and salads. Main dishes include minted lamb steak, fisherman's pie, fillet steak stuffed with pesto and wrapped in bacon.

RESTAURANT: With its arched ceiling, the spacious dining room recalls the glory of the Victorian era with chandeliers made from the original bell from the local church. There is a varied and interesting menu; starters can be duck and orange pâté with melba toast, wedges of Camembert with cranberry sauce, poached asparagus spears in a light white wine and olive sauce. Main courses may be beef Wellington, roasted breast of duck with juniper berry and redcurrant sauce. Steaks, fish and chef's "specials" are also available, plus a good selection of treats including hot apple strudel and chocolate-filled profiteroles.

OPENING TIMES:

Bar:

Monday - Saturday	12.00am -	3.00pm
	6.00pm -	10.00pm
Sunday	12.00am -	8.00pm

Restaurant:

Monday - Saturday	6.00pm -	10.00pm
Sunday	12.00am -	10.00pm

DIRECTIONS: Take A5 to town centre.

£ - £££

DICKENS CONNECTION

"There's beds here, sir", said Sam, addressing his master, Everything clean and comfortable. Very good little dinner, Sir, they can get ready in half an hour - pair of fowls, sir, and a weal cutlet; French beans, 'taturs, tart, and tidiness. You'd better stop vere you are, sir, if I might recommend. Take advice, sir, as the doctor said." The host of the Saracen's Head opportunely appeared at this moment, to confirm Mr. Weller's statement relative to the accommodations of the establishment, and to back his entreaties with a variety of dismal conjectures regarding the state of the roads, the doubt of fresh horses being to be had at the next stage, the dead certainty of its raining all night, the equally mortal certainty of its clearing up in the morning, and other topics of inducement familiar to innkeepers."

"Pickwick Papers"   Book II   Chpt. LI

The Warwick Arms Hotel

**17 High Street
Warwick
Warwickshire
CV34 4AT**

Tel : 01926 492 759
Fax : 01926 410 587

HISTORY: An impressive early 18th century coaching inn, the Warwick Arms was once the property of the Earls of Warwick and stands on the site of an earlier inn built in Tudor times, which burnt down in 1694. It is situated between the old town's East and West gates and is a short distance from the castle and the Lord Leycester Hospital.

BAR: The Town Bar is warm and comfortable, and portrays the Warwick of bygone days, and is just the place to relax and enjoy a quick snack. There's a selection of tasty freshly-made sandwiches and baguettes on offer, or hot jacket potatoes with a choice of savoury fillings.

RESTAURANT: In the elegant surroundings of the Westgate Restaurant, you are assured of a helpful and attentive service and the chef endeavours to provide new exciting dishes for the daily changing table d'hôte menu. Starters include Cajun breaded mushrooms with garlic mayonnaise or salad of prawns with cucumber vinaigrette. Main courses may be Brie and almond vegetable crumble or griddled chicken breast with bacon and Stilton. The à la carte menu offers something to suit all tastes, with starters such as spicy lamb in filo pastry and king prawns pan-fried in garlic, followed by main courses like rack of lamb with a herb crust and a rosemary jus, and pan-fried duck breast with a plum and ginger sauce. Delectable desserts may be baked Alaska, raspberry mousse or rhubarb and custard. The Sunday lunch menu features a choice of starters, followed by delicious roasts of beef, lamb or pork as well as chicken and fish dishes. To finish, there's a choice of desserts like pear charlotte, lemon meringue pie or ice cream sundae.

OPENING TIMES:

Bar/Restaurant:

Monday - Saturday	11.00am -	3.00pm
	6.00pm -	11.00pm
Sunday	11.00am -	3.00pm

DIRECTIONS:
M40 J15. Follow signs to town centre.

£ - £££

DICKENS CONNECTION

"Where shall we drive you sir?" said the post-boy. "You may drive me", said the single gentleman, "to the -" He was not going to add "inn", but he added it for the sake of Kit's Mother; and to the inn they went."

"The Old Curiosity Shop" Book II Chpt XLVII

Charles Dickens and Hablot K. Browne, his illustrator, stayed at the hotel in 1838.

North of England and Scotland

Scotland

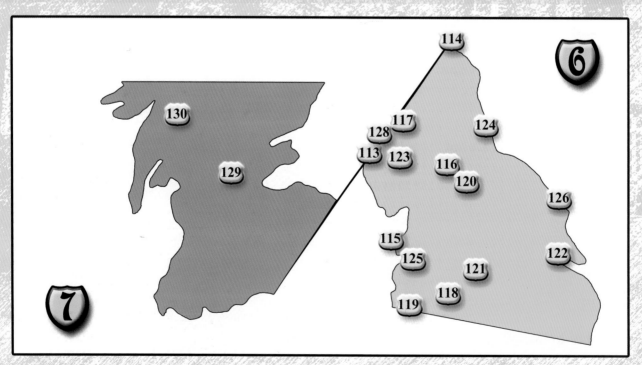

The Ship Hotel

Main Street
Allonby
Cumbria
CA15 6QF

Tel : 01900 881 017
Fax : 01900 881 017

E-mail : theshipallonby@aol.com

HISTORY: The attractive Ship Hotel is a grade II listed building, which was once a coaching inn on the Workington to Carlisle road, and dates back to the 17th century. With its soft sands and gently sloping beach, Allonby was a seaside resort as long ago as the 1750s. The area has been designated an "Area of Outstanding Beauty", with spectacular sunsets across the Solway Firth, which can be seen from most of the bedrooms. Charles Dickens and fellow novelist Wilkie Collins stayed at the hotel in the autumn of 1857 whilst on holiday in the north of England and the Lake District.

BAR: With its exposed beams and blazing fires on chilly days, the bar has a cosy atmosphere where you can enjoy various snacks and freshly-prepared good old fashioned pub food, or just a pint of real ale.

RESTAURANT: The small wood-panelled dining room offers a table d'hôte menu most weekends and specialises in Sunday lunches.

OPENING TIMES:

Summer:
Monday - Saturday	12.00am -	3.00pm
	6.00pm -	11.00pm
Sunday	12.00am -	3.00pm

Winter:
Tuesday - Saturday	12.00am -	3.00pm
	7.00pm -	11.00pm
Sunday	12.00am -	3.00pm
	7.00pm -	10.30pm
Monday	7.00pm -	11.00pm

DIRECTIONS:
From the A596 take the B5300 to the seafront.

🚗 🚻 🚭 ☺ ♿ ⬛▭ VISA £ - ££

DICKENS CONNECTION

"Allonby, gentlemen," said the most comfortable of landladies, as she opened one door of the carriage; "Allonby, gentlemen," said the most attentive of landlords, as he opened the other.
Thomas Idle yielded his arm to the ready Goodchild, and descended from the vehicle. Thomas, now just able to grope his way along, in a doubled-up condition, with the aid of two thick sticks, was no bad embodiment of Commodore Trunnion, or of one of those many gallant Admirals of the stage, who have all ample fortunes, gout, thick sticks, tempers, wards and nephews.
With this distinguished naval appearance upon him, Thomas made a crab-like progress up a clean little bulk-headed staircase, into a clean little bulk-headed room, where he slowly deposited himself on a sofa, with a stick on either hand of him, looking exceedingly grim."

"Christmas Stories"   Book II   Chpt. III   The Lazy Tour of Two Idle Apprentices.

The Kings Arms Hotel

Hide Hill
Berwick-upon-Tweed
Northumberland
TD15 1EJ

Tel : 01289 307 454
Fax : 01289 308 867

Web : www.kings-arms-hotel.com
E-mail : king's_arms.hotel@virgin.net

HISTORY: The Kings Arms Hotel has for many centuries been the principal inn of Berwick. This border town has been fought over many times by England and Scotland, and has been destroyed so often by border warfare that much of its documented history has been lost. However, the main stairway in the old Assembly Rooms is over 300 years old, and one of the most fascinating items of the inn's history is the old crockery bearing the Royal coat of arms with the inn's name boldly emblazoned below. Such crockery would not be used without Royal assent. In the cellars, there are four indentations on the cobbled ground. Three have been established as being ancient wells over 800 years-old, but the fourth appears to be a grave which has been left undisturbed. Incidentally, the body of James Ist of Scotland has never yet been found! In the garden, there is the shell of an 800 year-old granary and also a Saxon well dating back to 800 AD. During the Second World War, it is believed the hotel had been earmarked by Adolf Hitler as a main headquarters if the invasion had succeeded.

OPENING TIMES:

Garden Terrace:
    All week   10.00am - 6.00pm

Café Piazza:
    All week   12.00am - 2.00pm

II Porto di Mare:
    All week   6.30pm - 10.30pm

RESTAURANTS: There are three restaurants offering a huge choice of cuisine. Café Piazza has an intimate and inviting atmosphere, and is best described as a small corner of Italy and has a fantastic range of pasta and pizzas. The Garden Terrace is informal, with self-selection light meals and snacks, which can also be eaten in the medieval walled garden during the summer months.

II Porto di Mare is a modern-styled restaurant with a Mediterranean ambience and offers a wide and varied choice of exciting and innovative cuisine, with starters such as mussels and razor fish cooked with garlic tomatoes fennel and cream, asparagus wrapped with panchetta and deep-fried. Mains include marinated wild boar on a potato and apple charlotte, braised local venison, grilled red snapper on buttered saffron rice. Complete an enjoyable meal with a sweet such as tiramisu, or Dutch apple tart.

DIRECTIONS:
A1 to Berwick town centre.

£ - £££

DICKENS CONNECTION

CHARLES DICKENS
STAYED AT THIS HOTEL ON
26TH SEPT 1858 AND 25TH NOV. 1861
ON THE LATTER DATE
HE GAVE A READING
IN THE ADJOINING ASSEMBLY ROOMS

A statue of Charles Dickens showing him during his reading, stands in the Minstrel's Gallery to commemorate his visit.

The Imperial Hotel

North Promenade
Blackpool
Lancashire
FY1 2HB

Tel : 01253 623 971

E-mail :
imperialblackpool@paramount
-hotels.co.uk

HISTORY: In 1861, a syndicate was formed called The Blackpool Land & Building Company, who purchased the whole of the land on the northern seafront. On the 16th July 1863, plans were prepared for building a hotel; the site chosen was the most commanding position on Blackpool seafront. The following year, the directors were given authorisation to go ahead with the building of the hotel at a cost of no more than £15,000; the building took 2 years to complete. In the early years, the dreams of success came to nothing. Travelling facilities were poor, and visitors were not numerous enough for such a large hotel, and in 1897 the company went into voluntary liquidation for the purposes of reorganisation, and a new company was formed. Towards the end of the First World War, the Government took over the hotel and used it as a hospital for officers. Hundreds of famous guests have stayed at the Imperial ranging from royalty to stars of radio, theatre and television, including HRH Queen Elizabeth the Queen Mother to Bill Clinton, ex-President of the USA. The hotel has for many years been used for both the Labour and Conservative annual party conferences. The hotel bar is aptly named No. 10, and is steeped in political history and boasts it has served most of the country's Prime Ministers for the past thirty years.

BAR: For a quick snack and relaxing drink head for the No. 10 Bar where a selection of sandwiches are available.

RESTAURANT: There are two restaurants, the elegant and more formal Seaviews, which as the name suggests, has spectacular views and a fine à la carte menu; and The Palm Court, where you can enjoy the set menu. The pick of the menu from Seaviews includes starters of pan-seared scallops and black pudding hash brown, followed by sesame seared monkfish and braised shoulder of lamb. Pasta and salad dishes can either be taken as a first or main course. Round off your meal with imaginative and delicious puds such as strawberry soup and iced tiramisu. The Palm Court serves favourites such as sliced melon and fresh fruits and mixed seafood, followed by roast sirloin of beef and loin of pork, supreme of chicken and braised lamb, plus a Sunday lunch menu including mains of roast turkey, honey glazed gammon and mushroom ravioli.

OPENING TIMES:

Lunch (not Sat)	12.30pm -	2.00pm
Dinner (Mon-Fri)	6.30pm -	9.30pm
(Weekends)	6.00pm -	9.30pm

DIRECTIONS:
Take the A584 to seafront, North Shore.

£ - £££

DICKENS CONNECTION

My Dearest Georgy.
I send you this hasty line to let you know that I have come to this Sea-Beach Hotel (charming) for a day's rest. I am much better than I was on Sunday, but shall want careful looking-to, to get through the Readings. My weakness and deadness are all on the left side, and if I don't look at anything I try to touch with my left hand, I don't know where it is.

Part of letter written by Charles Dickens to Miss Georgina Hogarth whilst staying at The Imperial on 21st April 1869.

Ancient Unicorn Inn

Bowes
Nr. Barnard Castle
Co. Durham
DL12 9HN

Tel : 01833 628 321
Fax : 01833 628 028

Web :
www.ancient-unicorn.co.uk

E-mail :
management.unicorn@virginnet.co.uk

HISTORY: This is an impressive historic coaching inn built around a picturesque cobbled courtyard dating from 1545. The inn was an important stop on the old London/Carlisle mail coach road, where the horses could be changed and the passengers fed and rested. Five minutes walk away stood Shaw's Academy, which has now been redeveloped. Charles Dickens called it Dotheboys Hall. In the nearby churchyard are the headstones of the headmaster, Mr. Shaw (Wackford Squeers), and a boy called George Ashton Taylor, of Trowbridge, Wiltshire, who died suddenly aged 19 years in Mr. Shaw's Academy. Dickens later wrote: "I think his ghost put Smike into my mind on the spot."

BAR: The oak beams and the roaring fire add to the charm of the cosy bar where you can enjoy a wide range of snacks such as soup, freshly-made sandwiches and baguettes with a large selection of tasty fillings such as cheese, ham, chicken or egg. Also available, a full English breakfast.

RESTAURANT: Lit by candlelight in the evenings, the dining room offers a good choice of traditional English food freshly-prepared from local produce. The à la carte menu may include starters such as Stilton pear and duck pâté, prawn cocktail, or chicken goujons. Main courses may be red snapper, Whitby scampi, home-made game pie, or braised steak with red wine and tarragon. Daily specials include roasts of beef, pork, lamb, and chicken. Spoil yourself with a delicious sweet such as Boston Dome, strawberry gáteau, spotted dick or knickerbocker glory.

OPENING TIMES:

Bar/Restaurant:
All week   12.00am - 2.30pm
           7.00pm - 9.00pm

DIRECTIONS:
A66 about 15 miles from Scotch Corner.

Shaw's Academy - Dickens called it Dotheboys Hall.

DICKENS CONNECTION

Charles Dickens and Hablot K. Browne stayed at the inn in February 1838 and used the reading room to collate material for "Nicholas Nickleby".
Approximately six months after the book was published, a large majority of the Yorkshire schools closed down.

The County Hotel

9 Botchergate
Carlisle
Cumbria
CA1 1QP

Tel : 01228 531 316
Fax : 01228 401 805

Web : www.cairnhotelgroup.com

E-mail : mail@countyhotelcarlisle.com

HISTORY: This elegant hotel, built during the reign of King George III, overlooks the magnificent towers of King Henry VIII's historic Citadel. In the 1840s, the hotel was visited by Queen Victoria's mother, The Duchess of Kent. The County Hotel may be one of the newest hotels in Carlisle, but is actually situated in the oldest building in the centre of the city.

BAR: JR's is a newly-opened American-style bar and diner offering a very large selection of hot and cold food, such as soup of the day, potato skins with various fillings and a choice of delicious salads. From the grill, there is a variety of burgers made from fresh beef as well as chicken, chops and tender steaks, and a good choice of desserts.

RESTAURANT: The elegant Georgian dining room provides an attractive setting in which to enjoy some of the tempting dishes on offer. There is a table d'hôte menu as well as an extensive à la carte that has many starters with something to suit every taste, from Scottish smoked salmon to piping hot soup. Main courses include a good selection of fresh fish such as roulade of smoked salmon and lemon sole baked and served with a dill and citrus fruits sauce, or local rainbow trout baked with oregano and lemon juice. Also featured on the menu are steaks, chicken and pasta dishes, noisettes of lamb and duck. To finish, choose a tempting dessert such as chocolate or strawberry gáteau, hot plum sponge and custard or a choice of ice creams.

OPENING TIMES:

JR's Bar:

Monday - Friday	6.00pm	-	9.30pm
Saturday - Sunday	12.00am	-	3.00pm
	6.00pm	-	9.30pm

Restaurant:

All week	7.00pm	-	9.30pm

DIRECTIONS: In the town centre near the railway station and the Citadel.

🚌 🍴 ⊗ ⊜ ♿ 💳 VISA 📷 £ - £££

DICKENS CONNECTION

Charles Dickens sends his compliments to the Master of The Kings Arms at Lancaster and begs to say that he wishes to bespeak for tomorrow (Saturday) afternoon and night, a private sitting-room and two bedrooms; also a comfortable dinner for two persons at half past 5. Mr Dickens will be accompanied by his friend Mr. Wilkie Collins; and as Mr. Collins has unfortunately sprained his leg, it will be a great convenience to him to have his bedroom as near the sitting-room as possible. For the same reason, Mr Dickens will be glad to find a fly awaiting them at the station. They propose leaving here, by the mid-day train at 12..38.

Letter sent by Charles Dickens to Joseph Sly whilst staying at The County Hotel on 11th September 1857

George & Dragon

High Street
Cheadle
Cheshire
SK8 1AX

Tel : 0161 4282 857
Fax : 0161 4284 152

steak, rump steak, pork sausage and a fried egg, or maybe a grilled rump steak. There's also a choice of pasta dishes, or for something lighter choose a fresh salad -- prawn and tuna, Caesar chicken or spicy chicken and bacon. Tempting desserts include apple and blackberry crumble and chocolate dome cake.

OPENING TIMES:

Monday - Saturday   12.00am - 2.30pm

No food available on Sunday.

DIRECTIONS: Take M60 to J2 and follow signs to town centre.

HISTORY: The George and Dragon is an old 18th century coaching inn that faces the green and is situated in the centre of Cheadle at the junction of the Stockport Road and High Street. The inn was on the coach route that operated from Manchester to Wilmslow and places further south. Access to the old stable yard at the rear is clearly visible under the arch on the left-hand side of the building, and now serves as the inn's car park. But, like most of these old coaching inns, trade declined with the arrival of the railways.

BAR/RESTAURANT: An excellent selection of freshly-prepared hot and cold food is available in the comfortable dining room; Starters range from snacks to Cajun mushrooms, potato wedges, topped fries, filled rolls served with salad garnish, jacket potatoes and burgers served with chips and coleslaw. Main courses include Aberdeen Angus beef, lasagne, chicken tikka masala, fish and chips, and steak, mushroom and ale pie. If you have a hearty appetite, opt for the farmhouse grill -- lamb cutlet, gammon

DICKENS CONNECTION

Extract from Charles Dickens' diary whilst visiting Manchester, dated Wednesday November 7th, 1838.

Chaise to Cheadle	£1.	1s	0d
Hackney coaches		10s	0d
Bill at inn	4.	0s	0d
Boots		3s	0d
Porter		2s	0d
Fare to London	7.	13s	0d
Breakfast		7s	6d
TOTAL	£13.	16s	6d

Queen Hotel

**City Road
Chester
Cheshire   CH1 3AH**

Tel : 01244 305 000   Fax : 01244 318 483

Web : www.lemeridien.com
E-mail : kris.mathews@lemeridien.com

HISTORY: On the 21st of April 1860, the Queen Railway Hotel (as it was then called), opened its doors for receiving guests and soon became one of the premier hotels in Chester.   One of the main attractions was two little observation turrets situated at the top of the hotel from where an enchanting view of the city and surrounding countryside could be seen. Unfortunately, on the 26th November 1861, a fire broke out on the roof and spread to the upper floors and, sadly, the two observation turrets and the magnificent roof were burnt down.   But, in rebuilding, an extra floor was added extending the room capacity. The hotel's porters in bright gold and scarlet livery were granted permission to meet every train and would escort guests into the hotel through a covered arcade.   This structure now forms the entrance to the car park but was originally used for stabling horses. It is reported that every train was met well into the 1930s. This prestigious hotel has offered its hospitality to many famous dignitaries and celebrities including Cecil Rhodes, who stayed on many occasions, Lily Langtry, and Charles Dickens, who stayed here in January 1867 whilst on a reading tour of the North.

BAR/LOUNGE: The bars and lounges are comfortably-appointed and offer a good choice of hot and cold food, which includes a selection of triple decker sandwiches filled with roast beef and creamed horseradish, Highland smoked salmon and cream cheese.   There's also hot filled baguettes, garlic battered chicken goujons, omelettes, and sausages and mash. A delicious Victorian cream tea is served with sultana scones and preserves, smoked salmon and cucumber sandwiches, and freshly brewed tea.

RESTAURANT: The elegant dining room with its enchanting views of the gardens excels in fine dining.

To commence, there's a wide choice such as chicken liver parfait, red onion marmalade and toasted bloomer; citrus cured salmon with charred fennel and pimento salad. Interesting main courses include grilled pork loin, black pudding and caramelised onion gravy, or sweet roasted lamb rump, fondant potato and redcurrant jus. The sweet menu will be hard to resist with delights such as vanilla bavarois with brandy snap and mascarpone, and blueberry cheesecake.   To finish, there's a choice of fine cheeses including Shropshire Blue and Celtic Promise.

OPENING TIMES:

Bar:	All week	12.00am -	2.00pm
		6.00pm -	9.00pm
Restaurant:	All week	12.30pm -	2.00pm
		6.30pm -	9.30pm

DIRECTIONS: Opposite main line Railway Station, short distance from city centre.

£ - £££

DICKENS CONNECTION

Charles Dickens stayed at the hotel in January 1867. He gave readings from his works at the Music Hall, St. Werberg Street. He wrote to his daughter saying: "This seems to be a nice hotel." The weather was very severe that winter and Dickens goes on to say: "The hall is like a Methodist Chapel in low spirits, and with a cold in his head. I am now going to the fire to try to warm myself, but have not the least expectation of succeeding."

The Morritt Arms Hotel

Greta Bridge
Nr. Barnard Castle
Co. Durham
DL12 9SE

Tel : 01833 627 232
Fax : 01833 627 392

E-mail :
relax@themorritt.co.uk

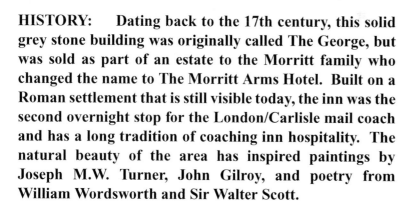

HISTORY: Dating back to the 17th century, this solid grey stone building was originally called The George, but was sold as part of an estate to the Morritt family who changed the name to The Morritt Arms Hotel. Built on a Roman settlement that is still visible today, the inn was the second overnight stop for the London/Carlisle mail coach and has a long tradition of coaching inn hospitality. The natural beauty of the area has inspired paintings by Joseph M.W. Turner, John Gilroy, and poetry from William Wordsworth and Sir Walter Scott.

BAR: The Dickens Bar has a wonderful happy atmosphere, inspired by the remarkable set of murals around the walls which were painted by John Gilroy for Major H.E. Morritt and are said to depict local characters celebrating in Pickwickian style. Hot and cold food is served in the bar such as ploughman's, cold meat platter, soup, and popular main dishes like fish and chips, steak and kidney pie cooked in Guinness, or spicy sausages.

RESTAURANT: For relaxed informal dining, opt for Pallet's Bistro. Starters may be grilled smoked salmon, or quenells of chicken liver parfit, followed by main courses such as collops of beef fillet set on provencale vegetables, and seared fillet of red snapper on a warmed leek, fennel and thyme compote. The oak-panelled Copperfield Restaurant is more formal, and offers an imaginative à la carte menu. Starters include confit of wood pigeon and Greta terrine. Main courses may be peppered roast cannon of lamb on garlic and walnut mash or collops of marinated venison. To finish your meal, try a cup of traditional "Morritt" bread and butter pudding, dark chocolate and spearmint mousse or a warm William pear and almond tart.

OPENING TIMES:

Bar/Bistro:
All week	12.00am -	3.00pm
	6.00pm -	9.30pm

Restaurant:
All week	12.00am -	3.00pm
	7.00pm -	9.30pm

DIRECTIONS:
A1 to Scotch Corner then take A66 about nine miles to Greta Bridge.

£ - £££

DICKENS CONNECTION

"We had for breakfast toast, cakes, a Yorkshire pie, a piece of beef about the size and much the shape of my portmanteau, tea, coffee, ham and eggs; and we are now going to look about us. Having finished our discoveries, we start in a post-chaise for Barnard Castle, which is only four miles off."

Extract from a letter sent by Charles Dickens to his wife. Dickens and Hablot K. Browne (his illustrator) stayed at the hotel in January 1838 whilst researching "Nicholas Nickleby"

The George Hotel

St. George's Square
Huddersfield
West Yorkshire.
HD1 1JA

Tel : 01484 515 444
Fax : 01484 435 056

Web :
www.brook-hotels.co.uk

E-mail :
thegeorge@brook-hotels.co.uk

HISTORY: The elegant George Hotel is situated on the main square in the town centre. It was built in 1851, and is a grade II listed Victorian hotel. The Italianate facade of the building complements the Huddersfield Railway Station, which is nearby. The hotel is famous as the birthplace of Rugby League Football; the meeting that founded it was held at the hotel in August 1895, and there's a fascinating display of memorabilia depicting the early days of the sport.

BAR: The bar menu won't disappoint with hearty portions of imaginative food, including smoked haddock kedgeree and courgette and red onion fritatta. Simpler dishes for a quick snack also feature, such as grilled steak baguette or a range of cold sandwiches.

RESTAURANT: The main restaurant is the perfect setting for a more formal dining experience. Tempt your taste buds with starters of chicken liver terrine with red onion marmalade or mixed mushroom feuilette. Mains include classics like braised lamb shank or venison sausages plus flavours from around the world -- try the deep-fried calamari, moules mariniére or Cajun spiced chicken breast. The extensive dessert menu includes white chocolate mousse with caramelised oranges in Grand Marnier syrup, warm apple pancakes with butterscotch sauce and fresh fruit salad with mandarin sorbet. On special occasions, such as St. Patrick's Day, there's a special themed menu, plus a good value three-course Sunday lunch.

OPENING TIMES:
All Week
   Bar: 12.00am - 9.00pm

   Restaurant: 12.00am - 2.00pm
                                   6.00pm - 9.30pm
<u>Restaurant is closed Saturday lunchtime</u>

DIRECTIONS: M62 take J24 to town centre; opposite Railway Station.

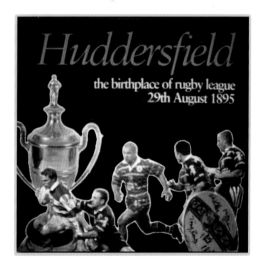

£ - £££

DICKENS CONNECTION

Charles Dickens stayed at the George on September 8th 1858 whilst on a reading tour.

The Quality Royal Hotel

170 Ferensway
Kingston-upon-Hull
Yorkshire
HU1 3UF

Tel : 01482 325 087
Fax : 01482 323 172

E-mail : admin@gb611.u.net.com

HISTORY: The Quality Royal Hotel (formerly called The Royal Station Hotel), was completed in 1849 in the Italianate style. Whilst visiting Kingston-upon-Hull in 1854, Queen Victoria, Prince Albert and five of their children, stayed at the hotel. In October 1990, the interior of the hotel was entirely destroyed; the only features to survive were the two main stone cantilevered staircases, and the external walls. The hotel re-opened in September 1992 fully reconstructed, with the ground-floor rooms a faithful copy of the original splendour of the Victorian era.

BAR/LOUNGE: The spacious lounge bar is just the place to relax and have a pint from the wide choice of fine ales available. Hot and cold food is also served and includes a selection of tasty sandwiches, omelettes, lasagne, chilli-con-carni, steak and ale pie, and fisherman's pie.

RESTAURANT: The attractive Royal Carver Restaurant offers a tempting selection of food. You can choose from either the à la carte, the carvery, or the set three-course menu. To start, try Brie wedges with redcurrant and cranberry chutney, gravadlax, and garlic mushrooms. Main courses may be peppered beef and cashew nuts, or fresh fillet of red snapper pan-fried with a fresh herb and butter sauce. From the grill, choose fillet or sirloin steaks with Diane, peppercorn or wild mushroom sauce, plus pasta and vegetarian dishes. To round off your meal, the sweet trolley offers a large choice of mouth-watering desserts.

OPENING TIMES:

Bar:	
All week	9.00am - 9.30pm
Restaurant:	
All week	6.30pm - 9.30pm

DIRECTIONS: Take the A63 and then the A1079 to town centre.

🚗 🚻 🚭 ☺ ♿ 💳 VISA 📷 £ - £££

DICKENS CONNECTION

My Dear Sir
I am very unwilling to trouble you, but I have been applied to by four friends to help them to purchase tickets, and obtain suitable places at the Dinner with which I am to be honoured next month in Liverpool.
The first is my eldest son.
The second is the Secretary of my Readings, Mr. George Dolby.
The third is Mr. Chorley, a distinguished musical critic and writer.
And the fourth is Mr. Charles Eliot Norton of Cambridge, Massachusetts, famous in America for his Italian scholarship.
If you can assist me gentlemen, I shall be greatly obliged to you.

Extract form a letter Charles Dickens wrote to Clarke Aspinall - British Transport Hotels, whilst staying at the hotel on the 9th March 1869.

The Mill Inn

Mungrisedale
Penrith
Cumbria
CA11 0XR

Tel : 01768 779 632

Web :
www.the.millinn.co.uk

E-mail :
margaret@the-millinn.co.uk

HISTORY: This is a charming 17th century coaching inn, part of which was once the local village mill; an original millstone still stands in the bar. The inn is set by the banks of the River Glenderamackin in the picturesque Mungriesdale Valley surrounded by stunning scenery, and close to the Blencathra Fell.

OPENING TIMES:

All week	12.00am -	2.30pm
	6.00pm -	8.30pm

BAR/RESTAURANT: The charming oak-beamed bar and restaurant with a roaring log fire, is the perfect setting in which to enjoy local produce freshly-prepared on the premises. There is a good choice of starters such as soup of the day, sautéed mushrooms with garlic, chives and cream, or grilled black pudding served on a bed of herb mashed potato with a grain mustard and bacon sauce. Main courses can include local Cumbrian lamb marinated in honey, garlic and mint, and finished on the griddle; sirloin or fillet steak, local Cumberland sausages, and home-baked beef and ale and steak and kidney pies. Fish dishes include Whitby scampi, and grilled fresh salmon with a mushroom, white wine and cream sauce. All main meals are served with plenty of seasonable vegetables and chips or new potatoes. On Sundays, a traditional roast is also served. Round-off your meal with a tasty home-made dessert such as apple crumble, hot chocolate fudge cake, or maybe a delicious ice cream. For something lighter, a choice of sandwiches and snacks are served in the bar.

DIRECTIONS:
Off the A66 Keswick to Penrith road.

£ - £££

DICKENS CONNECTION

Whilst on holiday in the North of England and the Lake District in the autumn of 1857, Charles Dickens and Wilkie Collins visited the Mill. On returning home, they wrote a story based loosely on their own experiences called A Lazy Tour of Two Idle Apprentices.

"Christmas Stories"   Book II   Chpt. II
Lazy Tour of Two Idle Apprentices

The Royal Station Hotel

Neville Street
Newcastle-upon-Tyne
Northumberland
NE1 5DH

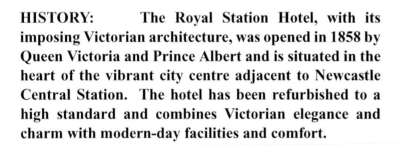

Tel : 0191 2320 781
Fax : 0191 2220 786

Web : www.royalstationhotel.com

E-mail : info@royalstationhotel.com

HISTORY: The Royal Station Hotel, with its imposing Victorian architecture, was opened in 1858 by Queen Victoria and Prince Albert and is situated in the heart of the vibrant city centre adjacent to Newcastle Central Station. The hotel has been refurbished to a high standard and combines Victorian elegance and charm with modern-day facilities and comfort.

BAR: The attractive and comfortable Empire Bar offers a very wide choice of hot and cold food such as freshly-prepared sandwiches with salad garnish and crisps, oven baked potatoes, tortilla wraps and pasta. Light meals can be mussels in a garlic cream sauce and old favourites like toad in the hole, steak and kidney pie, and chef's home made soup with a crusty roll. A selection of sweets and ice cream is available from the trolley.

RESTAURANT: In the elegant La Grille Restaurant, you can sample the culinary delights with the choice of à la carte or table d'hôte menus with starters such as choux buns filled with prawns and bound with a curried mayonnaise, or fanned melon with sorbet and mixed berries. Main courses might be pan-fried collops of pork fillet in a Stilton and port wine sauce, poached supreme of chicken with glazed shallots and a red wine meat glaze. Roasts are also available as well as a choice of steaks, and tempting desserts.

OPENING TIMES:

Bar:
All week   12.00am -   6.00pm
Restaurant:
All week   6.30pm -   9.30pm
Carvery:
Sunday   12.00am -   2.00pm

DIRECTIONS: A1 to city centre; adjacent to Newcastle Central Station.

£ - £££

DICKENS CONNECTION

My Dear Willis.
I return the cheque, duly signed.
I have just now walked over here from Sunderland (1 o'Clock), and have barely had time to look at the Room. It is new since we acted here-large-and capable of holding a good deal of money. I hope it will have a good deal to hold, tonight and tomorrow. The Let is a very good one, and we expect a large Take in payment at the doors.
You will be amazed to hear that we reaped very little profit at Sunderland last night!

Extract from a letter Charles Dickens wrote to W.H.Wills whilst staying at the hotel on 24th September 1858.

The Old Bull

**Church Street
Preston
Lancashire
PR1 3BN**

Tel : 01772 561 511

HISTORY: The Old Bull (formerly called The Bull & Royal) dating from about 1670, is the oldest hotel with a continuous record of hospitality in Preston. It has close associations with royalty; two of the greatest noble families in the country -- the Hamiltons and the Stanleys -- and High Court Judges, who stopped for food on their way to Lancaster Assizes. In 1701, the Duchess of Hamilton gave birth to a boy at the hotel. In gratitude for the care and attention shown to them and the safe delivery of his son and heir, the Duke presented the Preston Corporation with a silver gilt mace, which is still used on official occasions. In 1745, Bonnie Prince Charlie reached Preston on his journey south with his army and held a council at The Bull. Lord Stanley (later the 12th Earl of Derby) and one of the richest men in England, purchased the hotel in 1773, and some time later built the Derby Room, which he used for entertaining. The Earl was the founder of the Oaks and Derby horse races. In 1845, Charles Dickens stayed at The Bull whilst visiting Preston to get first-hand impressions of a strike at the cotton mills, which lasted 38 weeks. Dickens had for some time been gathering material for his novel, *Hard Times* and Coketown in the book, though based on Preston, was designed to satirize and emphasize the worst features of the Industrial Revolution.

BAR/RESTAURANT: The numerous pictures of old Preston around the walls add to the historic atmosphere of this old building. On the menu, there's a good choice of home-made food, ranging from snacks such as jacket potatoes with various fillings, burgers with salad and chips, and baguettes filled with prawns, tuna, cheese or ham, to something more filling. Choose from mixed grill, gammon or sirloin steaks, as well as old favourites like steak and kidney pie, battered fish and scampi.

OPENING TIMES:

Bar/Restaurant:
All week   11.30am - 4.00pm

DIRECTIONS: In the town centre.

£ - ££

DICKENS CONNECTION

On 22nd April 1868, whilst on a reading tour of the north of England, Dickens arrived at the Bull with his manager, George Dolby. The tour had been very strenuous and he was exhausted. He had an appointment to see his personal doctor who examined him and insisted the tour be cancelled immediately, as Dickens was on the brink of complete paralysis of his left side and apoplexy. He protested, but his doctor was adamant. The money for the reading had been paid in advance and would have to be refunded to the public, but the banks were closed. The Manager of the Bull, a Mr. Townsend, knew Dickens well and came to the rescue. He borrowed £120 from customers and friends and personally went to the Guildhall where Dickens was to give the readings, and refunded the money. Although Dickens had satirized Preston in Hard Times, he was overwhelmed by Townsend's kindness and the genuine sympathy of the people of Preston.

Dickens never gave another provincial reading.

Royal Hotel, Scarborough.
Sunday Eleventh September 1858.

My Dearest Georgy,   You will be surprised when I begin my letter by telling you that I have had an excellent opportunity of setting Katey quite right in the matter of Andrew. Coming home to the hotel at York from reading in that city on Friday night, who should I find, established in our room, but-Gordon! He had seen in Household Words where I was, and had come for a holiday, he said, intending to keep company with us for as far as Hull, and thence go back by Steamer. Arthur not having yet come up from the room, Gordon and I were alone; and he very soon took the opportunity of saying, with a kind of confidentially smirking satisfaction, that Andrew was uncommonly sweet indeed, upon a certain young lady at Gad's Hill, I immediately turned very grave, and said I had been quite uneasy about it, and had not known what to do. Gordon instantly changed, and asked "Why?" - "O! my good fellow," said I, "Why? Only because the difference is so obvious between a boy of 18, and a young woman of 19 or 20 -- and I like Andrew so very much, and should be so heartily ...

Addressee:

**Miss Hogarth
Gad's Hill Place
Higham
By Rochester
Kent.**

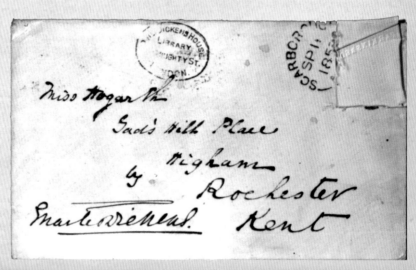

The Royal Hotel

St. Nicholas Street
Scarborough
North Yorkshire
YO1 2HE

Tel : 01723 364 333
Fax : 01723 500 618

E-mail : royalhotel@englishrosehotels.co.uk

HISTORY: The origins of the elegant Royal Hotel go back to 1725. It was known as The Long Room and this venue was used for reading, entertainment and meetings, and also by well-to-do visitors for social activities. It later became known as Donner's Hotel after the family who owned it. The name changed again to The Royal Hotel when Queen Victoria came to the throne. In the 1880s, Major Thomas Johnson became the manager on his retirement from a highly-successful and decorated career in the army; what sets him apart from any other officer in the British Army is the fact that he was one of only a few survivors from the valley of death and the ill-fated "Charge of the Light Brigade". Over the years, the hotel has been extended and has offered its hospitality to many famous people including Sir Winston Churchill and Edith Sitwell.

BAR: In the cosy and welcoming bar, you can enjoy a selection of snacks that include baguettes, sandwiches, pâté, soup and a selection of seafood.

RESTAURANT: The elegant dining room is the perfect setting for a special meal. Starters include galia melon filled with lemon sorbet and fresh strawberries, or cream of white onion soup flavoured with Wensleydale cheese. Main courses can be roast Yorkshire ham glazed with honey, mustard and Madeira sauce; fillet of fresh salmon lightly poached with prawn and cucumber sauce, plus beef and chicken dishes. To finish your meal, how about an irresistible dessert such as a meringue nest filled with exotic fruits, fresh cream lemon gáteau, or a selection of ice cream. The menu is changed daily.

OPENING TIMES:

Bar/Restaurant:
All week	12.00am -	2.00pm
	7.00pm -	9.00pm

DIRECTIONS:
On the seafront overlooking South Bay.

£ - £££

The Kings Arms Hotel

Market Place
Wigton
Cumbria
CA7 9NW

Tel : 01697 344 941

HISTORY: The Kings Arms was the premier inn standing in the centre of town and was on the well used coaching road between Carlisle and Whitehaven. The coach that operated the route was called The Jovial Sailor. When the railways came to the area, the proprietor of the Kings Arms ran a coach service from the hotel to the railway station. Charles Dickens stayed at the hotel in room 11. In 1948, a workman decorating the room supposedly found Dickens' signature by the window but papered over it. On telling the hotel owner, she requested that the paper be pulled back. Unfortunately, the signature came away with the wallpaper and was lost for ever.

OPENING TIMES:

Bar:
All week   11.00am - 11.00pm

🚗 ☺ **£ - ££**

DICKENS CONNECTION

"Wigton market was over, and its bare booths were smoking with rain all down the street. Mr. Thomas Idle, melodramatically carried to the inn's first floor, and laid upon three chairs (he should have had the sofa, if there had been one), Mr. Goodchild went to the window to take an observation of Wigton and report what he saw to his disabled companion. "Brother Francis, brother Francis," cried Thomas Idle, "What do you see from the turret?"
"I see," said Brother Francis, "what I hope and believe to be one of the most dismal places ever seen by eyes. I see the houses with their roofs of dull black, their stained fronts, and their dark-rimmed windows, looking as if they were all in mourning. As every little puff of wind comes down the street, I see a perfect train of rain let off along the wooden stalls in the market-place and exploded against me."

"Christmas Stories" Book II Chpt. II
Lazy Tour of Two Idle Apprentices.

BAR/RESTAURANT: The comfortable bar and dining area has a traditional pub atmosphere and offers a selection of freshly-made food. Choose from sandwiches and toasties with a variety of tasty fillings, or hot jacket potatoes with chicken and mushroom, cheese or tuna. There's a wide choice of main meals such as King's Arms "Challenge" mixed grill -- a bumper selection for when you have a hearty appetite. Alternatively, opt for lemon and pepper chicken, Cumberland sausages, fish, scampi, quiche or steaks -- or try the all-day breakfast. Main meals are served with chips, salad garnish and peas.

DIRECTIONS: Take A596 to town centre.

The Royal Hotel

55-103 Henderson Street
Bridge of Allan
Stirlingshire
FK9 4HG

Tel : 01786 832 284
Fax : 01786 834 377

Web : www.royal-stirling.co.uk

E-mail : stay@royal-stirling.co.uk

HISTORY: The Royal Hotel was built in the 17th century to accommodate the gentry who came to enjoy the therapeutic waters. It stands in an imposing position in the delightful Victorian spa town of Bridge of Allan, which boasts many magnificent buildings and the National Wallace Monument, a tribute to Scotland's greatest freedom fighter, Sir William Wallace. The hotel is an elegant testimony to Victorian times, with outstanding period features carefully restored and preserved to create a classic and relaxing ambience.

BAR/LOUNGE: For a light snack, morning coffee or afternoon tea, the Oak Room and King's Bar both provide a relaxed informal atmosphere to enjoy your food, which is served all day.

RESTAURANT: Enjoy a taste of Scotland in the award-winning Epicures Restaurant where produce such as beef, venison and fish is sourced locally. Choose from a light lunch menu, which includes dishes such as pan-fried fillet of salmon on a rich seafood chowder, or pasta served with mushrooms in a chervil and white wine sauce. For a special occasion, treat yourself to an evening meal. Starters can include pan-fried foie gras on a mango and grape chutney, beetroot cured gravadlax of salmon, or carpaccio of marinated Angus beef fillet, followed with dishes such as fillet of brill and rack of lamb with thyme-scented jus. There's also a char-grill serving steaks cooked to order with a choice of sauces and side orders. Round

off your meal with iced cranachan parfait with raspberry coulis, white chocolate mousse or passionfruit brúlée. The menu reflects all budgets with set price and à la carte options.

OPENING TIMES:

Bar/Restaurant:
All week 12.00am - 2.00pm
6.00pm - 9.30pm

DIRECTIONS: A9 to town centre. Near the Wallace Monument.

£ - £££

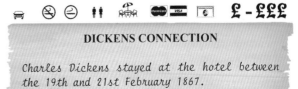

DICKENS CONNECTION

Charles Dickens stayed at the hotel between the 19th and 21st February 1867.

King's House Hotel

Glencoe
Argyll
PH49 4HY

Tel : 01855 851 259
Fax : 01855 851 216

Web :
www.kingy.com

E-mail :
kingshouseglencoe.com

HISTORY: The King's House was built in the 17th century, and is on the main route between Glasgow and Fort William, and is said to be one of Scotland's oldest licensed inns. The scenery of mountain and loch is some of the most spectacular in the country. The building was used as a barracks for troops of King George III after the battle of Culloden in 1745, hence the name King's House. It was the task of the troops to keep the highlanders under subjection and also to capture the elusive Bonnie Prince Charlie. At the turn of the 20th century, work began on the Black Water Reservoir, and the hotel was the last port-of-call for the hundreds of workmen making their way to the dam via the Devil's Staircase at Alt-na-feidh. Many men got lost and perished on the hills.

BAR/RESTAURANT: With its beamed interior and open fires the inn has a charming rustic atmosphere. It offers a good selection of freshly-prepared local produce; starters include smoked venison, soup of the day and smoked mackerel. Main courses can include seasonal game like grouse, pheasant and venison, as well as fresh salmon, chicken dishes and steak pie -- served with potatoes and vegetables or chips and salad. Finish your meal with a home-made dessert such as Irish coffee pudding, strawberry cheesecake or chocolate cake.

OPENING TIMES:

All Week

Bar/Restaurant	12.00am -	8.30pm
Dinner	7.00pm -	8.30pm

DIRECTIONS:
Off the A82. The nearest station is Bridge of Orchy (14 miles).

£ - £££

DICKENS CONNECTION

"One stage of ten miles, over a place called the Black-mount, took us two hours and a half to do; and when we came to a lone public house called the King's House, at the entrance to Glencoe - this was about three o'clock - we were well nigh frozen. We got a fire directly and in twenty minutes they served us up some famous kippered salmon, broiled; a broiled fowl; hot mutton ham and poached eggs; pancakes; oatcake; wheaten bread; butter; bottled porter; hot water, lump sugar, and whiskey; of which we made a very hearty meal."

"Extract from a letter Charles Dickens wrote to John Forster, his friend and biographer, dated 9th July 1841, whilst touring Scotland.

AMERICAN NOTES

It took nearly a quarter of a century for Dickens to give America a second chance. His first visit in 1842 had not been the great success that he had hoped, even though the publication of *Pickwick, Oliver Twist* and *Nicholas Nickleby* had given him international recognition as an author, and brought him success and adulation across the Atlantic. As well as being a private holiday "to walk on the soil I have trod in my daydreams many times", he also embarked on an extensive tour looking for new audiences for his work and new material for forthcoming books, including *American Notes*, which had already been commissioned by his London publisher, Chapman & Hall. There was a great deal of curiosity in Europe about the lifestyles of our American cousins, and Dickens saw the huge potential in more ways than one of this largely untapped market. Although there was no denying his popularity amongst the American public and his great enjoyment of the social and literary circles in which he mixed, the highlight being a private interview with the rather dull but mild President John Tyler, who was surprised at Dickens being so young, he soon realized that the American dream he'd envisaged didn't really exist; he'd set sail from Liverpool expecting to find some kind of utopia, but was greeted by a country with many of the same social, political and economic problems that he'd left behind at home. To add to his disillusionment, he opened the debate at every opportunity on the need for proper international copyright protection and was shocked by how divided the publishing industry was on the subject. Dickens often bemoaned the injustice of never deriving sixpence from an enormous American sale of his books.

Ironically, when he decided to return in 1867, financial gain was largely at the heart of the decision. It had taken five months for Dickens to finally make up his mind to go again, but despite failing health and having just completed fifty reading tour dates in Britain, a six-month tour of America was just too good an opportunity to miss. Apart from the lure of many social invitations, Dickens felt that such a tour would also help to reclaim some of the riches he'd lost in royalties from his novels over the years. His new business manager, George Dolby, helped secure Dickens eighty-four venues, which entailed a great deal of travelling, much entertaining and many stop-overs at hotels. The whole tour was a sell-out from Boston to Baltimore and up to Buffalo on the border of Canada. At one of his readings there were more than 2,000 people present. It brought in £1,200 profit per week and made the equivalent in today's terms of one million pounds in total, culminating in a grand dinner at Delmonico's restaurant in New York, which was hosted by the American media.

CHARLES DICKENS TRAVELS TO USA 1842

Cleveland, Ohio April 25th 1842

The great English novelist, Charles Dickens, arrived here today on the latest stop of his American tour. At the tender age of 30 he has already published three great works - *Pickwick Papers* (1837), *Oliver Twist* (1838) and *Nicholas Nickleby* (1839). Dickens and his wife landed in Boston in January and on 14th February they were feted at the Boz Ball, a gala named after the author's nom de plume which was held at the Park Theatre. The city's most eminent people paid $10 a head to attend. Famed for his crusading attacks of London Slums, Dickens spoke well of America, but has already embraced two new causes. He has denounced slavery and is pressing for international copyright laws to prevent the pirating of author's works.

Other Events in 1842

★ Massachusetts State Law bans under 12's from working more than 10 hours a day in factories

★ Far West explored by Freemont and Kit Carson

★ End of second war with Seminole Indians

★ The anesthetic, ether, first used by Dr. Crawford Long for non-dental operations

★ Captain S. Mallett arrives in French warship in Honolulu demanding broad powers for Islands Catholics

★ First time milk is shipped by rail

★ America's first grain elevator built

★ First successful underwater telegraph cable laid by Morse between Governors Island and Castle Garden

★ Opening of the first wire suspension bridge across the Schuylkill River

St. Louis

Lebanon

Louisville

Cairo

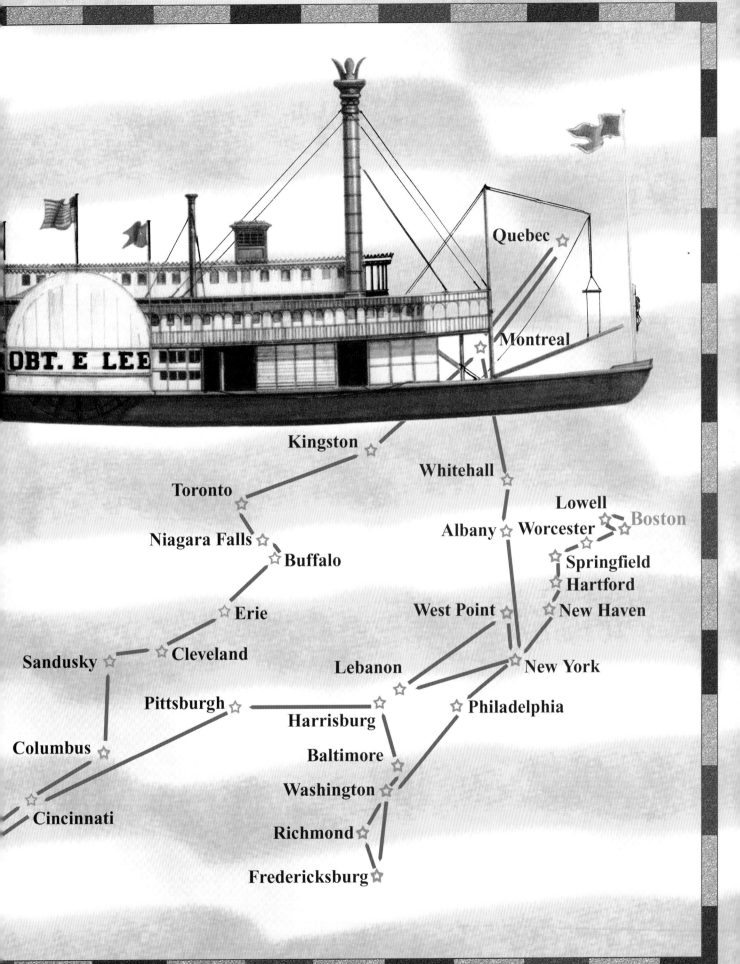

ROBT. E LEE

Quebec

Montreal

Kingston

Whitehall

Toronto

Lowell

Boston

Niagara Falls

Albany

Worcester

Buffalo

Springfield

Hartford

Erie

West Point

New Haven

Sandusky

Cleveland

Lebanon

New York

Pittsburgh

Philadelphia

Harrisburg

Columbus

Baltimore

Washington

Cincinnati

Richmond

Fredericksburg

All at sea

When Dickens and his party set sail one cold, foggy January morning in 1842, the American chapter of his life was just beginning. His party, including his wife Catherine, had boarded the SS Britannia at Liverpool, bound for Boston. A "state room" had been prepared for the much-fêted Dickens, who had just completed a triumphant trip to Edinburgh the previous June and was enjoying the success of his latest novel, *Barnaby Rudge*. He hoped to receive the same kind of reception on the other side of the Atlantic, and expectations were high. Writing to Lewis Gaylord Clark, editor of the New York *Knickerbocker Magazine*, Dickens says: "I cannot describe to you…the glow into which I rise, when I think of the wonders that await us, and all the interest I am sure I shall have in your mighty land." The crossing was a stormy one and took 18 days. Life on board wasn't easy either, even for the captain's famous guest, who coped with the tedium -- and the seasickness -- by reading, resting and walking on deck. When he was well enough to eat, the stewardess would serve dishes such as steaming baked potatoes, roasted apples, boiled leg of mutton with green capers, cold ham and salt beef. On other occasions, Dickens recalls "a store of hot meats of various kinds – not forgetting the roast pig, to be taken medicinally". He was also rather partial to brandy and water for its health-giving properties too! The menu may have been fairly predictable and plain, but the voyage was far from plain sailing; just outside Halifax, Nova Scotia, the Britannia ran aground on a mud flat, which was blamed on pilot error and sudden fog. It arrived safely in Boston on January 22; as the ship docked, well-wishers and the American media were waiting to catch a glimpse of just one of the eight-five passengers on board – the famous English novelist, Charles Dickens. Dickens himself couldn't have wished for a more enthusiastic welcome in "Boz-town" (as it was nicknamed by jealous New Yorkers); the city had done him proud.

"Knots of people stood upon the wharf [Liverpool], gazing with a kind of 'dread delight' on the far-famed fast American steamer; and one party of men were 'taking in the milk,' or, in other words, getting the cow on board; and another were filling the icehouses to the very throat with fresh provisions; with butchers'-meat and garden-stuff, pale sucking-pigs, calves' heads in scores, beef, veal, and pork, and poultry out of all proportion." *American Notes*

The Steamship Britannia was the first of four sister ships commissioned by Samuel Cunard for the British and North America Royal Mail Steam Packet Company known from the beginning as The Cunard Line. She was a wooden paddle steamer built at Greenock in 1840. In 1849, after 40 crossings, she was sold to the North German Federation and converted into a frigate and renamed the Barbarossa, later converted into a hulk at Kiel where she was finally scrapped in 1880.

Wined and dined across America

Soon after arriving in Boston, and with the press hot on his heels, Dickens retreated to the Tremont House Hotel where he "sat down to dinner in ten minutes…and a capital dinner it was". Later that first evening, he took a stroll around Boston's snow-covered streets with the Earl of Musgrave, whom he'd met on the voyage. Dickens spent several weeks touring Boston, and much of his time involved attending many

Tremont House, Boston

private dinners and parties; he was also guest of honour at a public dinner on February 1st, hosted by the "Young Men of Boston". Writing to one of his English friends, he remarks: "There never was a King or Emperor upon the Earth, so cheered, and followed by crowds, and entertained in Public at splendid balls and dinners." As well as enjoying such privileges, he also got to experience some typical customs, including visiting a bar and sipping cocktails like Mint Julep and Gin-sling; Dickens also tried some typical culinary delights, such as cranberries, hot stewed oysters, and "beef steak…swimming in butter and sprinkled with the blackest of all possible pepper". He even wrote humorously about the aphrodisiacal powers of oysters because they were such a staple food on the American plate. On a more serious note, Dickens' social conscience never deserted him despite his celebrity status; he also found time to visit institutions including an asylum, an institute for the blind, several factories, and a seamen's chapel. Dickens left Boston on February 5th and headed for New York, travelling by rail and steamboat. He

New York Bay

Carlton Hotel - New York

visited some New England towns along the way, including Lowell, Hartford (where a dinner was held for him) and New Haven, before arriving in "the beautiful metropolis of America". He stayed at the grand Carlton Hotel on Broadway. Every town in America wanted to entertain him publicly and New York society was eager to outdo its rivals, particularly Boston. A highlight of the stay was a ball held in his honour called the Boz Ball, which was at the Park Theatre on February 14th. Organized by a committee of prominent citizens, no detail was overlooked; three thousand people attended, paying five dollars per ticket. "The bill of fare for supper, is, in its amount and extent, quite a curiosity," Dickens wrote in a letter to Forster, but he also found it to be "the most splendid, gorgeous, brilliant affair".

Park Row - New York

On the menu

As well as using five thousand plates and four thousand glasses for the banquet, one hundred and forty people were employed to get the refreshments ready, plus over sixty waiters. Dickens was completely overwhelmed by this "extraordinary festival" as he called it, and no wonder. Highlights of the menu included:

50,000 oysters; 10,000 sandwiches; 40 hams; 76 tongues; 50 boned turkeys; 50 pairs of chickens; 25 pairs of ducks; 2,000 mutton chops; 150 gallons of Madeira wine; 350 quarts of jelly and blancmange; 300 quarts of ice cream plus two barrels each of almonds, apples and oranges. To round-off the meal, they drank more than a barrel of port and 60 gallons of tea.

Hitting the headlines

Details of the banquet appeared in many national papers. Dickens kept the cuttings and sent them with letters to family and friends.

WELCOME

TO

CHARLES DICKENS.

THE BOZ BALL.

TO BE GIVEN

UNDER THE DIRECTION OF A COMMITTEE

OF

CITIZENS OF NEW YORK,

AT THE

PARK THEATRE,

ON THE EVENING

OF

THE FOURTEENTH OF FEBRUARY NEXT.

NEW YORK:

J. C. House, Printer, 88 Barclay-street.

1842.

United States Hotel - Philadelphia

Past and present Philadelphia

The next stage of Dickens' journey took him by rail and then ferry to Philadelphia. He arrived on March 5th and stayed at the United States Hotel. By now, he was becoming disillusioned with many aspects of American life and, in Philadelphia, was particularly alarmed by the solitary-confinement prison system. Haunted by what he saw, he went on to write about it in *A Tale of Two Cities*. In a letter to Forster, written from Philadelphia on March 6, he also condemns the odious practice of using spittoons and chewing tobacco. "There are spit-boxes in every steam-boat, bar-room, public dining-room, house or office, and place of general resort, no matter what it be…In every bar-room and hotel passage the stone floor looks as if it were paved with open oysters," he wrote.

Congress and the club-house

From there, he went on to Washington via Baltimore in Maryland and met up with his admirer Edgar Allan Poe. Dickens took rooms at Barnum's Hotel but his visit here was overshadowed by the fact that he was waited on by many slaves at a dinner he attended. When writing in *American Notes*, he says: "Though I was, with respect to an innocent man, its presence filled me with a sense of shame and self-reproach." He arrived in the capital on March 9th and stayed at Fuller's Hotel

Barnum's Hotel - Baltimore

before being wined, dined and toasted by the most elite and powerful, including President Tyler himself, who invited Dickens to lunch at his mansion. Dickens likened the building to "an English club-house". With such influential new friends, Dickens also took every opportunity to lobby members of Congress about the need for an international copyright law.

The President's house from the river

The only statute in the world of Charles Dickens is to be found in Clark Park, Philadelphia. Here, Dickens' great grandson, Cedric Charles Dickens and his wife, Elizabeth, pose proudly by the memorial.

Elizabeth and Cedric by the only statue of my Great-grandfather in the world

Cedric Charles Dickens

Trains, plains and picnics

Dickens' American adventure really began when he left the comforts of Washington, and the Eastern seaboard, and headed south and west. The railroad system was in its infancy, so thousands of miles were covered by stagecoach or river travel, which he often found exhausting, distressing and even frightening. Although Dickens attended receptions en route and could often look forward to a fine meal and a comfortable bed at night, this wasn't always the case. Staying at Planter's House in St Louis, he talks of drinking "large glasses of milk with blocks of ice in them as clear as crystal".

The Planters House - St. Louis

He adds: "Our table was abundantly supplied indeed at every meal. One day, when Kate and I were dining alone together, in our own room, we counted sixteen dishes on the table at the same time." However, the logistics of negotiating vast open prairies and waterways interspersed with deserted and decaying settlements meant that no set meal times could reasonably be adhered to. Therefore, many meals were eaten on the move, such as something simple like "wheat bread or chicken fixing" or taken al fresco. Sometimes, the stage would stop at a public house to water or rest the horses,

St. Louis

but there wasn't always much food available for the hungry and weary travellers on board, and they'd often have to make do with ham and coffee. Dickens complains about the empty larders of many of the establishments he visited, but he also enjoyed many hearty meals and "stagecoach banquets" during his travels. On a canal boat journey from Harrisburg to Pittsburgh, he recalls: "At about six o'clock all the small tables were put together to form one long table, and everybody sat down to tea, coffee, bread, butter, salmon, shad, liver, steaks, potatoes,

Cincinnati Landing

pickles, ham, chops, black puddings, and sausages. 'Will you try,' said my opposite neighbour, handing me a dish of potatoes, broken up in milk and butter."

Dickens went on to Cincinnati, Louisville, Cairo and up the Mississippi. Picnicking on the plain, he says: "Out came two baskets with roast fowls, buffalo's tongue, (an exquisite dainty, by the way,) ham, bread, cheese, and butter, biscuits, champagne, sherry; lemons and sugar for punch; and an abundance of rough ice." He then stopped briefly in Lebanon on April 20th, and dined at the The Golden Lamb, which is still in existence today (see page 152).

The final stages of his six-month sojourn in America took him northwards again, retracing his steps through Ohio before crossing the border to "the English side" – Canada – where he rested and holidayed for a month before returning home in June.

The Golden Lamb - Lebanon

CHARLES DICKENS' READING TOUR 1867/8

With the American and British flags above
his head, he stood up and began:
"The story of my going again... is very easily told..."

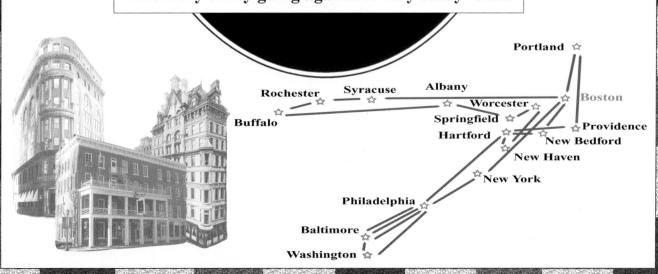

America revisited

The tour of 1867-8 began with a celebratory dinner in London and ended with one in New York. One week before departure, Dickens was honoured at a farewell banquet at Freemasons' Hall, which was presided over by his close friend, Lord Lytton. Over 450 guests, many from the literary world, attended the lavish affair and as Dickens entered the throng he was greeted with waving handkerchiefs from the floor and galleries; a roar rang through the hall and the band struck up a rousing march. Dickens was so overwhelmed by his reception that he was reduced to tears and needed to take "a desperate hold" of himself before making his speech. With the American and British flags above his head, he stood up and began: "The story of my going again…is very easily told…"

The Cunard ship, Cuba, left Liverpool on November 8th 1867. Dickens was allocated the second officer's cabin, which opened directly on to the deck. Worried about getting seasick again, he was able to get plenty of fresh air during the voyage and, it is said, found that eating baked apples regularly helped keep nausea at bay. He took plenty of books

Freemasons' Hall - London

with him to pass the time and worked on the reading tour. On many occasions, he chose to dine in his small cabin rather than having to be the celebrity 'on show' in the public dining room. There was months of that kind of adulation to come.

Boz back in Boston

His arrival in Boston in the early evening of November 19th mirrored the welcome he'd received all those years before; one reason he'd returned was to meet the many new friends upon whom he had never looked. If he thought that the public's enthusiasm for his literature was in any doubt, now was the time to think again. In honour of his visit and status, the streets had been swept and some public buildings had been given a lick of paint. While Boston's famous guest was being whisked off to the Parker House Hotel to rest and eat, queues began stretching for over half a mile in the streets outside his publisher's office as fans tried to get tickets for his readings. Some people even slept out overnight on straw mattresses to avoid disappointment; money would change hands to secure a place nearer the front of the queue. Boston considered itself to be the cultural capital of America

Parker House Hotel - Boston

and Bostonians couldn't get enough of the superstar Boz. Within hours, the four initial Boston readings were sold out with receipts taken of $14,000; Dickens was such a draw that speculators were attempting to bulk buy tickets to sell on for huge profits. Dickens mania had soon gripped America.

Food for thought

In spite of this, the man himself had decided to keep a lower profile this time. Rooms had been prepared for Dickens' stay at the Parker House (see page 148) and his every whim was catered for. His manager, George Dolby, was determined to keep his charge out of the limelight for a number of reasons, so Dickens was assigned a private waiter and mainly dined in his apartment. There would be no repeat of the round of public banquets that had been a feature of his first American adventure and even Dickens agreed, admitting that he found them tedious. But he had other things on his mind too: he wanted to concentrate fully on getting his performances right; so much so that he spent hours alone in his room working on the logistics of the tour and learning the scripts by heart. Dickens remained rather reclusive, preferring to prepare for his readings, but he did find time to dine out and "grasp the hands of many

faithful friends", or he would entertain in the privacy of his hotel. His 'inner circle' included publisher James T. Fields and his wife Annie, the poet Henry Wadsworth Longfellow, members of The Saturday Club, and George Putnam, who'd acted as his secretary on the first trip. When a journalist asked him why he hadn't been seen much in public, Dickens replied: "I am come here to read. The people expect me to do my best, and how can I do it if I am all the time on the go?" Dickens had a point, but deep down he was also concerned about the state of his health and wanted to avoid unnecessary stresses and strains. He'd left England exhausted from a reading tour and with a swollen, painful foot. Significantly, he travelled with a medicine box containing laudanum, ether, sal volatile and a form of digitalis for the heart. Then no sooner had he arrived on American soil, he got a bad cold and catarrh. Ahead of him lay a gruelling work schedule of four readings per week and a total of 84 performances.

By the time Dickens opened on December 2nd at Tremont Temple, the cold had turned into influenza. He read extracts from A *Christmas Carol* and *Pickwick* to great acclaim, then after three more performances, moved on to New York for six more readings, including Doctor Marigold, at the famous Steinway Hall. Friends were starting to get worried about his poor appetite. He was often tired, low, and felt homesick. Fields comments: "He was accustomed to talk and write a good deal about eating and

drinking, but I have rarely seen a man eat and drink less…Both at Parker's hotel in Boston, and at the Westminster in New York, everything was arranged by the proprietors for his comfort, and tempting dishes to pique his invalid palette were sent up at different hours of the day; but the influenza had seized him with a masterful power."

The show must go on

The bitter cold weather didn't help either; a concoction of brandy, rum and snow, called a 'Rocky Mountain Sneezer' was concocted for him, but to no avail. He tried all kinds of remedies, but just didn't get any better. In a letter to his sister-in-law, written from New York, he says: "My cold sticks to me, and I can scarcely exaggerate what I undergo from sleeplessness. I rarely take any breakfast but an egg and a cup of tea – not even toast or bread and butter. My small dinner at 3, and a little quail or some light thing when I come home is my daily fare; and at the hall I have established the custom of taking an egg beaten up in sherry, and another between the parts, which I think pulls me up…"

After readings in Brooklyn, held in the novel surroundings of a chapel, the "show" crisscrossed towns and cities throughout the winter, before arriving in Washington at the beginning of February. Dickens had completed half the tour, but was "dead beat" and often in a state of collapse after each performance. He rose late and ate little solid food, mainly existing on just beef tea and soup. His foot was still extremely painful and lame and he was now using a hot mustard poultice to soothe his bad chest. It was as much as he could do to rally for each reading, which he always did brilliantly feeling that "no man had a right…to break an engagement with the public, if he were able to get out of bed". But the logistics of the tour were now being left to Dolby to ease the burden.

In the money

The money kept rolling in, and Dickens' presence in America undoubtedly helped with the sales of his collective works. In one transaction, £10,000 was banked with Coutts in London. So he kept going, travelling to new places and some familiar ones from 1842, including Baltimore, Syracuse, Rochester and Buffalo. To his great relief, Canada, Chicago and the west had been removed from the itinerary. Commenting on his decision to miss Chicago, he found his sense of humour again. "I would rather they [the fans] went into fits than I did."

The last goodbye

Dickens arrived back in Boston for his farewell readings on April 13th and then moved on to New York to close the tour. He was glad that he would soon be back on the other side of the Atlantic with his family again. Spring had arrived; the tour had been a triumph; he was a

Lady Burdett-Coutts of Coutts Bank

rich man; he'd tied up many lose ends, both personally and professionally; and a passage home on the steamship, Russia, had been booked. At last, he had made peace with himself and America. But despite all this, Dickens was still feeling poorly and had aged a great deal in the six months he'd been away. He even commented that he'd noticed that his hair had started falling out and "what I don't lose is getting very grey". Dickens was in so much pain that he arrived late and left early for the dinner at Delmonico's (see page 150). Whether or not revisiting America had been worth it, only time would tell.

A fistful of dollars

Some of the receipts from the tour that made Dickens a fortune:

New Bedford $1640 : Rochester $1906
Springfield $1970 : Providence $2140
Albany and Worcester $2400
Last night in Washington $2610
Philadelphia $2910
Four readings in Brooklyn $11,128
Farewell nights in New York $3298
Farewell nights in Boston $3456

DOLBY:-"Well, Mr. Dickens, on the eve of our departure, I present you with $300,000, the result of your lectures in America."

DICKENS:-"What ! only $300,000 ! Is that all I have made out of these penurious Yankees, after all my abuse of them ! Psh no ! Let us go, Dolby !"

Following in his footsteps:

Professional actor Gerald Charles Dickens, Dickens' great great grandson, has revived the unique and mesmerizing reading tours, taking to the stage in Britain, America and Australia. He is seen standing beside a picture of Charles Dickens at the Omni Parker House in Boston on a recent reading tour.

Omni Parker House

60 School Street
Boston
Massachusetts 02108
USA

Tel : (617) 227-8600
Fax : (617) 742-5729

Web : www.omnihotels.com

HISTORY: Entrepreneur Harvey Parker bought a cheap eating-house in the 1830s and turned it into a fine restaurant called Parker's. But his ambition was to create a grand, first-class hotel based on the European style. After making a great success of the eaterie, a site was acquired in School Street to turn his plans into reality. Construction began on the hotel in 1854 and the Parker House opened its doors a year later to rave reviews. The five-storey building provided the ultimate in opulence and comfort with its splendid marble façade, thick carpets and fashionable horse hair beds. The hotel installed the first passenger lift in Boston and meals and room service were provided 24 hours a day. It soon became the place to be seen, and was the preferred venue for many gentlemen's clubs, including two notables: The Literary Club and The Magazine Club. The intention of the monthly gatherings, which were held on a Saturday, was to produce a magazine, and *The Atlantic Monthly* was the result. When the magazine was published, the clubs merged to form The Saturday Club, which was based on the old literary 'salons' – a place where the leading writers and thinkers of the day could meet to dine and enjoy each other's company. The Parker House didn't disappoint and the guests could look forward to lavish seven-course feasts lasting many hours. A typical menu of the day would have included dishes such as oysters, green turtle soup, baked cod in claret sauce, compote of pigeons, partridges with truffles and jelly, blue-billed widgeon, woodcock, black duck, calf's foot and Madeira jellies, charlotte russe, lemon and apple pies, pears, oranges, peaches, walnuts, almonds and raisins. In his book, *Charles Dickens as I knew him*, George Dolby talks of trying other exciting new dishes at Parker House, such as sweet potatoes, yams, stewed terrapin and "green corn – the latter a most delicious vegetable which I soon learned to gnaw off the cob".

Dickens became a regular guest of the club during his stay at the hotel on the tour and wrote for the magazine. His great friend, Henry Longfellow, was a member of this elite circle. On one memorable occasion, Dickens plied members with his recipe for English gin punch and asked for a reinforced table to be placed in his suite (room 338 of the old hotel) to hold the heavy punch bowl.

Dickens found the hotel and service perfect, and said so in letters written from the hotel. In one to his daughter, he comments: "This is an immense hotel, with all manner of white marble public passages and public rooms. I live in a corner, high up, and have a hot and cold bath in my bedroom (connecting with the sitting room) and comforts not in existence when I was here before. The cost of living is enormous, but happily we can afford it." When he was well enough, Dickens would embark on long walks starting from the hotel, and would often be accompanied by his closest friends. Dressed flamboyantly, he was hard to miss in his brightly-coloured coat, shiny boots and striped cravat. The idea for a "Great Walking Match" between himself and the manager of his publishing house was hatched at Parker House. After covering more than twenty miles on the jaunt, which Dickens lost, he graciously hosted a dinner at the hotel to "celebrate".

The current Omni Parker House has expanded over the years and now has 530 bedrooms and 21 suites, but it retains its reputation for superb food and luxurious accommodation, and is a favourite amongst Dickens fans to this day and the Dickens family. Dickens memorabilia can be found throughout the hotel, including the original marble mantelpiece and walnut mirror from his room. Who knows how many times he practised his lines and characterizations in front of it?

RESTAURANT:

As well as a selection from the grill, including juicy steaks, veal chops and rack of lamb, the restaurant menu is an eclectic mix of American and international flavours. You can choose from home-grown favourites, such as baked Boston Schrod, scallops Nantucket and New England lobster. Dishes as diverse as three cheese ravioli, classic roast duck with caramelized apples or chicken masala also feature. For pudding, you must try Boston cream pie, which is the official dessert of the State of Massachusetts. Other tempting treats include cheesecake, chocolate torte and cranberry apple cobbler. For a more informal snack, head to the Last Hurrah bar or relax by the fire in Parker's bar.

OPENING TIMES:

Lunch:	Monday - Friday	11.30am - 2.30pm
	Saturday - Sunday	12.00am - 2.30pm
Dinner:	Monday - Saturday	5.30pm - 10.00pm
	All week	2.30pm - 10.30pm

DIRECTIONS: On the corner of Washington Street and School Street.

DICKENS CONNECTION

Charles Dickens stayed at the hotel on his second visit to America in 1867.

Delmonico's

56 Beaver Street
New York 10004
USA

Tel : 212-509-1144
Fax : 212-509-3130

Web : www.delmonicosny.com

HISTORY: The original Delmonico's or "Del's" was the realisation of a dream for Swiss-born brothers Giovanni and Pietro Del Monico. Sensing the need for an up-market eaterie in Manhattan, they started with a small café and pastry shop on William Street, and then went on to open the Restaurant Francais next door. Both establishments were destroyed by a fire in 1835 but, undaunted, and with a growing culinary reputation, the brothers opened the doors of Delmonico's on Beaver Street in 1837. With magnificent stone pillars at the entrance, excavated from the ruins of Pompeii, a grand interior, and a 100-page gourmet menu, Del's soon established itself as the ultimate "dining club" amongst café society. In 1862, the restaurant appointed its first celebrity chef, Charles Ranhoffer, who stayed for thirty years and created two classic signature dishes – Baked Alaska and Lobster Newburg. So when the American press barons were looking for a venue to hold Dickens' farewell dinner at the end of his reading tour, it could only be at one place: Delmonico's. Invitations were sent out to over 200 members of the press, and the lavish banquet was held on April 18th 1868 from 5pm. Guests enjoyed over 40 sumptuous and exquisitely-prepared dishes using the finest ingredients, including consommé with chicken timbales, braised lettuces, poached salmon garnished with lobster, spinach velouté in pastry, and maraschino cherry savarin. Host Horace Greeley, founder of the *New York Tribune*, had been determined to change Dickens' mind about America, and saw this occasion as the perfect opportunity for reconciliation. Ironically, Dickens still had a poor appetite and was in great pain, but all this had been forgotten as the proceedings got under way. He was completely humbled and overwhelmed by the reception he'd received on this occasion and throughout his stay. Having ridiculed America and even its cuisine in *Martin Chuzzlewit* and *American Notes,* he stood up and made a significant speech in which he acknowledged that "amazing changes" had taken place since his first visit in 1842. He issued what amounted to a retraction and promised that no further copies of those two books would go to press without a postscript referring to his change of heart. Resentment, anger and disillusionment had given way to a lasting impression of "unsurpassable politeness, delicacy, sweet temper, hospitality, consideration… and respect". He also thanked them for allowing him some privacy due to the nature of his work and the condition of his health.

BAR:

For a lighter meal, you can dine in the 2000 Bar and Grill, which serves club sandwiches, burgers and snacks, such as crispy fried shrimps or calamari. Power breakfasts are also a favourite for the early risers, many of whom work on nearby Wall Street. Choose from a traditional fry-up to pancakes or Eggs Benedict.

RESTAURANT:

The current Delmonico's has been refurbished to reflect its former glory and the menu features many classics from Dickens' day. Although the restaurant isn't owned by the Del Monico family, it still enjoys a great reputation for fine food. It is primarily a steak house, but fish dishes also feature strongly including sesame crushed tuna, oysters Rockefeller, Maryland style crab cakes, clam chowder and the famous Lobster Newburg. Other mains to tempt the taste buds can range from imaginative salads to veal chops, country roast chicken, roast rack of lamb and a selection of steak dishes. There's also a choice of vegetables and potatoes on the menu. The wine list abounds with over 800 choices from around the world. Diners can capture a taste of the past in Dickens' Alcove, which can accommodate up to 90 people.

OPENING TIMES:

Monday - Friday	7.00am - 10.00pm
Saturday - Sunday	Private parties only

DIRECTIONS: Landmark building on the corner of 14th Street and 5th Avenue.

DICKENS CONNECTION

Dickens attended a banquet at Delmonico's on 14th April, 1868 at the end of his tour.

The Golden Lamb

27 South Broadway
Lebanon
Ohio 45035
USA

Tel : (513) 032-5065

Web : www.goldenlamb.com

HISTORY: The inn is reputed to be the oldest in Ohio and has witnessed two centuries of American history. The original log tavern on the site was built in 1803 and given a licence as a "house of entertainment". It was replaced with a brick building in 1815 but many additions were made to the structure over the years to accommodate guests as it flourished during the heyday of stagecoach travel. Charles Dickens arrived outside The Bradley House, as it was called then, with his party, including Catherine, her maid and his secretary. The horses needed changing, so they stopped here for dinner on their way to Columbus. Annoyed that he couldn't get a drink, Dickens recounts the fact in *American Notes*: "We dine soon after with the boarders in the house, and have nothing to drink but tea and coffee. As they are both very bad, and the water is worse, I ask for brandy; but it is a temperance hotel, and spirits were not to be had for love or money." After eating, Dickens greeted local dignitaries before resuming his journey. As well as Dickens, other famous guests have included Mark Twain and 10 American presidents. There is now a Charles Dickens room, decorated in Victorian style for guests to enjoy, and the hotel is also listed as a Shaker museum. Visitors are encouraged to explore the rooms, including the bedrooms when available, to view the collection of Shaker furniture and artefacts.

RESTAURANT: With four public rooms and five private dining rooms, the inn can cater for all tastes and occasions. You can choose from light snacks, such as pâté, crab cakes or shrimp cocktail. More substantial mains are also served, and many have a traditional mid-western flavour. Highlights include Indiana duckling with orange sauce and wild rice; prime rib of beef; Butler County turkey with giblet gravy, and braised lamb shank. All meals are served with a choice of potatoes, vegetables and relishes. There's a selection of home-made puddings to follow, plus an extensive wine list featuring European and American wines.

OPENING TIMES:

Monday - Saturday	11.00am -	3.00pm
	5.00pm -	9.00pm
Sunday	12.00am -	3.00pm
	4.00pm -	8.00pm

DIRECTIONS: The inn is situated on the corner of Broadway and Main Street.

DICKENS CONNECTION

Charles Dickens stopped at the inn for dinner on the 20th April 1842

Second Helpings

Whether it's the ritual of having a Sunday morning drink in your local, lazing away an afternoon over a pub lunch, or pulling out all the stops for a gastronomic feast, nothing beats the combination of good food, good wine and great company. It's a sentiment that has stood the test of time: in *Martin Chuzzlewit*, Dickens describes the jovial appearance of the landlady of the Blue Dragon inn and remarks on how the "hearty participation in the good things of the larder and the cellar" can have "healthful influences". And not just for publicans! Therefore, as well as the 101 eateries already featured in the guide and to give you as much choice as possible -- Dickens would have approved -- we have squeezed in even more places with a Dickens connection. Due to pressure of space, the details are brief, so please telephone the eateries on the "menu" for specific information.

Ye Olde Red Cow
71 Long Lane
London EC1A 9EJ

Tel: 0207 6060 735

Christmas Stories

The Chequers
Church Street,
Lower Higham Kent
ME3 7LB
Tel: 01474 822 794
Three Jolly Bargemen
Great Expectations
Chpt. XVIII
(Now rebuilt)

The Admiral Penn
59 Beech street
Deal Kent

Tel: 01304 374 279

'Reprinted Pieces'
Out of Season
(Called Admiral Benbow)

The Ship
14 The Street
Cobham Kent DA12 3BN

Tel: 01474 814 326

Frequented by Dickens
when walking home to
Gad's Hill Place

Upper Bell
1 Chatham Hill
Blue Bell Hill Village
Chatham Kent
Tel: 01634 861 149

'The Mystery of Edwin Drood'
Called The Tilted Wagon
Chpt. XV

Saracens Head
42 Broad Street
Bath Avon BA1 5LP
Tel: 01225 426 518

Charles Dickens stayed whilst
visiting Bath.

The Royal Hotel
Market Place
Kettering Northants
Tel: 01536 520 732

Charles Dickens stayed at the
original hotel whilst on his
reading tours.
(Now rebuilt)

Royal Kings Arms
75 Market Street
Lancaster LA1 1HP
Tel: 01524 32 451

Charles Dickens stayed here in
1857 & 1862 whilst on his
reading tours
(Now rebuilt)

DICKENS CHRONOLOGY

1812 Charles John Huffam Dickens born February 7th, at 393 Old Commercial Rd, Landport, Nr. Portsmouth.
Father John Dickens. Mother Elizabeth Dickens (neé) Barrow.

1817 Family move to 2, Ordnance Terrace, Chatham.

1821 Dickens begins education at William Giles School, Chatham.

1822 Family move to 16 Bayham St, Camden Town, London.

1824 John Dickens arrested for debt, sent to Marshalsea Prison. Dickens working in Warrens' Blacking Warehouse, Hungerford Market, London.

1826 Dickens attending Wellington House Academy, Hampstead.

1828 Dickens meets Maria Beadnell.

1829 Dickens learns shorthand and becomes freelance reporter at Doctors' Commons.

1831 Becomes a Parliamentary reporter

1833 First published story: 'A Dinner at Poplar Walk'.

1836 April 2nd. Marries Catherine Hogarth.
Sketches By Boz
Pickwick Papers 1836/7

1837 January 6th. Charles Culliford Dickens born. Family move to 48 Doughty Street, London.
Oliver Twist 1837/8

1838 March 6th. Mary (Marie) Dickens born.
Nicholas Nickleby 1838/9

1839 October 29th. Kate Macready Dickens born. Family move to 1, Devonshire Terrace, Regent's Park, London.

1840 Master Humphrey's Clock
The Old Curiosity Shop

1841 February 9th. Walter Landor Dickens born.
Barnaby Rudge

1842 First trip to America.

1843 Martin Chuzzlewit 1843/4
A Christmas Carol

1844 January 15th. Francis Jeffrey Dickens born. Family move to Italy.

1845 October 28th. Alfred D'Orsay Tennyson Dickens born.

1846 *Daily News* established.
Dombey and Son

1847 April 18th. Sydney Smith Haldimand Dickens born.

1849 January 16th. Henry Fielding Dickens born.
David Copperfield 1849/50

1850 *Household Words* established.

1851 August 16th. Dora Annie Dickens born. Family move to Tavistock House, Bloomsbury, London.

1852 March 13th. Edward Bulwer Lytton Dickens born.
Bleak House 1852/3

1854 Hard Times

1855 Little Dorrit 1855/7

1856 Dickens purchases Gad's Hill Place, Higham, Kent.

1858 First public readings. Separates from Catherine.

1859 *All The Year Round* established.
A Tale of Two Cities

1860 Great Expectations 1860/2

1862 Second series of public readings.

1864 Our Mutual Friend

1865 Dickens in Staplehurst rail crash.

1866 Third series of public readings.

1867 Second trip to America.

1868 Last series of public readings.

1870 Edwin Drood Started
June 9th. Dickens dies.
June 14th. Dickens buried in Poets' Corner in Westminster Abbey.

HOMES WHERE DICKENS WROTE HIS MAJOR NOVELS

**13/15 Furnivals Inn, Holborn, London
(Dec 1834 - April 1837)
Sketches by Boz - Pickwick Papers**

**48 Doughty St.
London
(April 1837 - Dec 1839)
Pickwick Papers
Oliver Twist
Nicholas Nickleby
Barnaby Rudge**

**1 Devonshire Terrace,
Regent's Park, London.
(Dec 1839 - Nov 1851)
Master Humphrey's Clock
Barnaby Rudge
Old Curiosity Shop
Martin Chuzzlewit
Christmas Carol
Dombey and Son
David Copperfield**

**Fort House, Broadstairs, Kent
(July 1849 - June 1870)
David Copperfield - Bleak House**

**Tavistock House, Bloomsbury, London
(Nov 1851 - July 1860)
Bleak House - Little Dorrit
Hard Times - David Copperfield**

**Gad's Hill Place, Higham, Kent
(Feb 1857 - June 1870)
Tale of Two Cities - Great Expectations
Our Mutual Friend - Edwin Drood**

Charles Dickens' died here at Gad's Hill Place, Higham, Kent on June 9th 1870.

The words spoken by the Dean of Westminster at Charles Dickens' memorial service in Westminster Abbey on June 19th 1870.

If any of you have learned from his works the eternal value of generosity, purity, kindness and unselfishness, and have learned to show these in your own hearts and lives, these are the best monuments, memorials and testimonials of one who loved with a rare and touching love, his friends, his country and his fellow man.

Ron Cook, Cedric Dickens, Reg Edmondson and Peter Park
outside The Dickens House Museum, Doughty Street, London. - 13th June 2003.

ACKNOWLEDGEMENTS

The authors would like to extend their grateful thanks to the undermentioned for their kind co-operation and for the information supplied : All of the hotels, inns, pubs and restaurants included in the book -- Bath and North East Somerset Libraries and Archives (page 65) -- Boston Herald USA (147) -- Cambridge County Council Libraries and Heritage -- Cheltenham Public Libraries (58) -- Dickens House Museum. Doughty Street, London. (Front cover, 1, 8, 9, 144, 135, 136, 137, 138, 139, 140, 141, 142, 143, 146 & 147) -- David Salmon. Alver Picture Promotions (57 & back cover) -- Egmont Books (132 & 133) --The Library and Museum of Freemasonry (144) -- Guildhall Library (73 & 74) -- Kingston-upon-Hull Libraries and Archives. -- Medway Council Archives and local Studies Centre. -- Norfolk County Council Cultural Services. -- Post Office Museum. (72) -- Oxford University Press. Pilgrim Edition. Letters of Charles Dickens (35, 52, 70, 78, 87, 99, 115, 117, 122, 124 & 130) -- Surrey County Council History Centre. -- West Malling Public Library.

A special thanks to Maureen Edmondson for her many hours of work and dedication.

RESEARCHERS

Ardwyn & Enid Davies -- Jean Cook -- Ken & Mildred Edmondson -- Jason Hayward -- Phil Mitchell -- Norman & Mary Sharpe -- Dennis Turnbull -- Ginette Park -- Dick & Marilynne Zimmerman (USA)

FURTHER READING AND REFERENCES

The Life of Charles Dickens. 2 vols., 1876 by : John Forster
Dickens A Biography. Hodder & Stoughton. 1988 by : Fred Kaplan
The Omni Parker House. 2001 by : Susan Wilson
Dickens. Sinclair-Stevenson Ltd. 1990 by : Peter Ackroyd
Dickens on America and The Americans. Harvester Press. by : Michael Slater
Charles Dickens As I Knew Him. 1912 by : George Dolby
The Miricle of Pickwick. Doughty Street Publications. by : Cedric Dickens & Alan Watts
American Notes. Chapman & Hall. by : Charles Dickens

BRIEF HISTORY of the ROCHESTER DICKENS FELLOWSHIP
By Paul J Allen (BA) RDF Chairman

Over one hundred and thirty three years after the birth of Britain's greatest novelist, Charles Dickens, his memory still lives on thanks to his wonderful books and short stories plus the eternal interest of thousands of members across the world, of the fellowship that bears his name -- The Dickens Fellowship; It is a tribute and testimony to the universal appeal Dickens' writings transcending almost one hundred and seventy years of such change and innovation since his first novel appeared that a body devoted to those writings and the author's life exists. Thus it is not surprising due to his continued popularity that the local branch of the Dickens Fellowship in Rochester is celebrating its 100th Anniversary. For Dickens not only attracts world-wide appeal through his imaginative story-telling but also gains an undaunting following due to the interest in his era, the Victorian age. Combining his genius, with the honest and imaginative manner with which he observed and expressed this period, made him a great novelist and a social observer as well.

In 1903 B. W. Matz presenting his first report as the Hon Secretary of the Dickens Fellowship to the first AGM (London), was able to speak of a year of very productive activity. The Fellowship, founded on 6th October 1902, had already sprouted other branches, in this country and around the world. In all, in its initial year fifteen branches had been given their charters, acknowledged by the parent Fellowship branch with a membership comprising 3,464 members world-wide.

Among those original fifteen was Rochester with all its Dickens associations. Charles had spent his early life in the Medway Towns writing about Rochester and the surrounding area in his works. Therefore, it is not surprising, an early branch of the newly formed Dickens Fellowship would be established in the city so close to his heart. Twenty years later, so established was the branch, Rochester Mayor, R.W. Dale, commenting on the branch and Dickens said: "The city is better known the world over because he lived here and spoke of it....I am glad the city had such a Fellowship and that it was so flourishing. We have several organisations of which we are proud of, but there would be something entirely lacking if the city had not the Fellowship. I wish them great and increased prosperity." It has prospered and continues to do so.

The RDF was established on Tuesday 26th May 1903, at a meeting held in the Guildhall council chamber by kind permission of the Mayor. Among those present were Rochester society's turn of the 20th century notable elite. Soon after the branch's conception, a programme of meetings was established. In 1931 the first Rochester Dickens Pageant took place. Many of the international Dickens Fellowship conferences were held in Rochester and significantly we were hosts for the 'Millennium Dickens Fellowship Conference', in which our slogan was 'Taking Dickens into the 21st Century'. So can be said of the local branch itself. For as we celebrate our 100th Birthday, possibly the most active of the UK branches, we are taking ourselves into the new millennium with a membership of over 200 and numerous future planned activities. Thus we are very much a branch with a long history which is also looking forward and developing for the future. Anniversaries bring the past through to the present. Bound together by fellowship, loyalty and love of Dickens, members of yesteryear can proudly sit with us at our meetings. Without them, we would not be celebrating our '100th Anniversary'.

Today our world is as diverse from our founders as Dickens must have been to them, yet a common thread persists. Perhaps this is the attraction, an important aspect to our 'fellowship' but it is only one of many. Dickens is 'The Inimitable' -- the 'Fellowship' is inimitable among literary societies. Trusting this has been illustrated in this brief 'RDF History', I hope too anyone on joining the RDF might reflect: "It is a far better thing that I do now than I have ever done." (*Tale of Two Cities*). You too can be a part of the branch's history when it celebrates its 200th Anniversary by joining us now.

ROCHESTER FELLOWSHIP - PROJECT RESEARCHERS: Sylvia & John Blundell -- Tony & Margaret Riddle -- Freda Man -- Terry & Sandra Wickens -- Colin Benson -- Peter & June Smith -- Graham Smith -- Thelma & Wilfred Grove -- Paul & Irene Allen -- Jo Armstrong -- Diana Stewart -- Simon Wickens -- Caroline Guillon -- Peter & Sylvia Sherrif -- Joe Beard USA -- Therese Saxton USA

Index

Job Trotter Encounters Sam in Mr. Muzzle's Kitchen